MW01680360

A COWBOY'S *whispered* PSALMS

A COWBOY'S *whispered* PSALMS

KIP SAWDY

Tate Publishing & *Enterprises*

A Cowboy's Whispered Psalms

Published by Tate Publishing & Enterprises, LLC
127 E. Trade Center Terrace | Mustang, Oklahoma 73064 USA
1.888.361.9473 | www.tatepublishing.com

Tate Publishing is committed to excellence in the publishing industry. The company reflects the philosophy established by the founders, based on Psalm 68:11,
"The Lord gave the word and great was the company of those who published it."

Cover design by Kellie Southerland
Interior design by Joey Garrett
Photography by Arnica Spring Photography, www.arnicaspring.com

Published in the United States of America

ISBN: 978-1-61566-498-6
1. Poetry / Inspirational & Religious
2. Religion / Christian Life / Personal Growth
10.02.16

ACKNOWLEDGMENTS

I want to thank the Father for accepting me for who I am. I praise him that he loved me so much that he sent his only son, Jesus, to die on the cross for me. I cannot comprehend the love the Father has for me and every person on earth. I only hope that my life and death will glorify him and the kingdom of heaven!

There are a few individuals I want to acknowledge. The first is my identical twin brother. Kent, you are my best friend, and we have been through thick and thin together. Good times and bad. Most people can't understand the connection and unconditional love we have for each other, but that is something we just can't explain. I know I can count on you the most. I love you and praise God for bringing you into this world slightly before me! I know how lucky I am to have you, even though I do not show it all the time. I love you, bro! Can't imagine life without you!

To my grandparents, Jerry and Mae, thank you for always being there for me when I needed someone or something. You guys always listened to me, and I never felt judged by you but always felt love from the both of you. I love you guys so very much! I thank God for giving me wonderful grandparents.

Dad and Mom, I thank God for you. I love the both of you so very much and thank you for being there for me. Both of you have taught me a great deal about life. Dad, I've adopted your gentle spirit. I remember when I was young and asked you why you thought you survived the Vietnam War, and your reply was that maybe you were supposed to help bring us into the world so one of us kids would find the cure for cancer. You, Kent, and I were in your yellow Ford truck when I asked this. We were pulling out of the garage of the old Casper house. Well, I've found something better than a cure for cancer and that is the cure for sin—Jesus! I believe the Lord protected you throughout your life to give me life, for he had a plan much greater than you or I could ever imagine. I love you and thank God for you!

Mom, I thank you for your unbelievable organizational skills and a calling to get things done. Because of your organization and love, you have made sure our health was in mint condition. You went above and beyond in the care of Kent's and my diabetes. We had some sore bottoms when we snuck treats; I now thank you for that. Thank you also for financially helping me when it was needed. You have a good and giving heart and bless many people with what you can, but your knowledge and wisdom are priceless! I remember when we were young and living in the old Blackrock house, you made some fresh chocolate chip cookies and had them on the counter. I tried to talk Kent into sneaking some with me late one night, but he declined. So I went ahead and got some for myself. The next morning, you came into the room and asked who got into the cookies. I blamed Kent right off the bat, and he blamed me. You said you were going out to talk with God to see who really did it. I didn't believe you, but a few minutes later, you came in with the way all of it unfolded almost down to the exact words. That planted a huge seed in my heart. If you could talk to God like that and hear him, I wanted to. So I thank you for hearing me that night and saying God told you. That really caught my attention! I love you very much!

Tammy, I thank you for not being a hypocrite when you gave your life to the Lord. You planted a huge seed in my heart when Mom and Dad were finalizing the divorce, and you made that one phone call. You were crying and said that you didn't want me to go to hell. I was offended and said I was fine with God. But the road I was on was not leading me toward the kingdom of heaven. Your heartfelt phone call means so much to me. You not only witnessed to me by your words, but by your actions. I watched you like a hawk from that point on, waiting to see if I could catch you messing up to call you a hypocrite. That opportunity never happened for me. You lived it and applied it! Bless you! I love you very much and thank God for a wonderful sister!

To my Aunt Maxine and Uncle David, thank you for persisting with me and witnessing to me. Thank you for helping me when times were tough in Denver. You could not afford to send me money to get down there to see you, but in faith you guys sent money because you heard from the Lord. Thank you for being sensitive to the Holy Spirit, for that sensitivity saved my life! I love you guys very much.

To the rest of my family, thank you and God bless

you all, for each and every single one of you had a major part in who I am today.

Last but not least, thank you James and Jamie for all of your hard work editing all my mess-ups, along with everyone else who helped. It is appreciated! God bless you all!

TABLE OF CONTENTS

PREFACE

I find myself in a constant battle—the battle between my flesh and my spirit. If I satisfy my flesh, I foreclose on my soul. When I satisfy my spirit, I receive heavenly favor. The battle is constant, and I find the only way to win is to put the things that satisfy my flesh to death. To walk away from pleasure now is to put favor in my case when the judge puts eternal court into session. The verdict *is* up to me. Knowing the reward and the punishment ahead of time only gives me more zeal to satisfy the one who has made an eternal home for me.

—Kip Sawdy

INTRODUCTION

I hope when you read poems of prayer you are inspired—inspired to live a life closer to the Lord, to bless one another, to give a helping hand, or simply to love others and treat them the way you want to be treated. I hope this book will also make you sit back and think about what is important in your life. Is the life you are living glorifying God? Do you realize how blessed we are in America and what God has done for you?

I believe a good writer should stir people's emotions, emotions such as anger, love, sorrow, excitement, and sadness, just to name a few. Or perhaps a good writer should just have the ability to make people think deeply, hopefully deep enough to make them want to change their ways. I hope I was able to capture the right words and put them in the right sequence that will bless you and make you think. I, Kip Sawdy, did not write this book. I give all glory to God, for I know this gift of writing is a generous gift from him, and I hope I'm able to keep it by glorifying the one who has distributed the gift. The Lord deserves all credit and praise, for he wrote this book.

This book is *not* to inspire religion, but to inspire a personal relationship with the Father and his Son.

Many poems were inspired by experiences. Some were inspired by talks with friends and family, TV, or emotions I was going through at the time. Writing these poems helped me release those emotions. I felt bottled-up for so long; I was ready to explode. I felt and heard things from the Holy Spirit that I could not shake off. So this book was a way to release what I felt the Spirit was speaking to me. A company asked if I could write a prayer for bull riders that they could use on T-shirts. I said, "Sure, it will be a few weeks before I could finish it." Needless to say, I was done with that poem within a couple of hours, and it is included in this book. It's called "A Bull Rider's Prayer." Original, huh?

I never could write poems before, but God blessed me with these poems within a month, give or take. Like I said, God wrote this book; he just used me to deliver!

Some statements are rather bold and straightforward. I believe people should not beat around the bush. I want to know people's motives and what is on their minds straight up. When you are straight up with people, there are no guessing games going on.

A person, in my opinion, who speaks the truth in a discerning way is a person with great integrity. This is rare and almost extinct. But no one is perfect, except Jesus himself!

I hope and pray this book will inspire you to live the life God asks us to live in his Word. Your salvation, blessings, and rewards depend on how much of his Word you follow. Your eternal future is secure the second you accept Jesus as your Lord and Savior and believe he is God's only Son, that he died on the cross for your sins, was raised from the dead three days later, and sits at the right hand side of God. If you do not believe this and think you get to heaven by works or any other way, your eternal future is in deep trouble!

Let's not be hypocrites, fellow Christians. Let us worry about how we live our lives according to the Word and not how everybody else lives theirs. If you don't, you're stepping in Jesus' position and judging before the proper time. Besides, not one of us will live a life even remotely close to the life Jesus lived.

I speak about subjects most people do not want to hear about because they do not want to hear the truth, for the truth will offend them. I've heard it said, and I believe it with all my heart: "I would rather offend you into heaven than comfort you into hell."

NOT MY TIME

In my mouth was a loaded .357.
I planned to make my way to heaven.
I had been living in sin.
My hopes had all grown dim.
I prayed for one more chance
Before I took my last dance.
God heard me pray;
Then he showed me his way.
At first it seemed like a dream;
A dream, it wasn't. I realized that was Satan's scheme.
I got into God's Word
And realized my living had been absurd,
I asked Jesus to take my soul,
So I could get out of this hole,
But it wasn't my time,
And I couldn't take something that wasn't mine.

I was living in Denver, Colorado, years ago and fighting terrible depression. I had moved down there for business. I grew up in the Rocky Mountains in Wyoming and the city life was too much for me, besides the point that I had no idea what to do with my life.

I thought a relationship would cure me, and I prayed that God would bring me a girlfriend. I asked the Lord to be my Savior two years earlier but didn't have a full understanding or knowledge of what to do with my newfound salvation. I meant it when I asked Jesus into my heart, but I didn't have anyone to direct me or coach me along the new road I wanted to follow.

So a young lady came into my life, and I thought it was God sending her. Temptation got the best of us. We moved in together, and we all know what that means. *Sin!* My new relationship didn't cure my depression or even cure my loneliness. The fact is, it all got worse. A relationship will not cure anything if we have struggles inside of us. Most people will blame others for their failure, but the truth is we need to face the root of the problem and ask the Lord to heal us and come to grips with any kind of past that may be haunting us. But instead we hide it under fake smiles and confidence. I have found that it is okay to be weak, to ask for help. Do yourself and others a favor; deal with those issues and find out who you are in Christ Jesus, because it is not fair to bring others into your life when you are not ready for them.

Our relationship was a tough one for this young lady. It hurt her to see what I was going through, but she had no idea how to help. I asked for help and tried to tell her what was going on, but I didn't know how to put the feelings into words.

God heard my prayers, and he used her to help me. During the course of our relationship, she was introduced to Jesus as her Lord and Savior. She prayed and asked him into her heart, despite the way we were living. *Praise God!* Nevertheless, we kept living in sin, but we both felt convicted that it was wrong. She was the one that took that conviction and did something about it.

I had to make a trip to California and had planned to stay there for a week. A couple of days after I was there, she called and said that she was moving out. Needless to say, things for me at that time were not going *my* way. I now praise God for what she did at that time because that was the only way to wake me up. Before I left California, I rededicated my life to the Lord with a little more knowledge than before.

A short time had passed, and I was wallowing in my sorrows, doing a lot of praying, and begging God to help. To my dismay, he was helping me, but at the time, I couldn't see it. One night the hurt was so bad that I decided to take my life. I went into my room and grabbed my Smith and Wesson .357. I went into my dining area and dropped to my knees. I was in tears and felt so very empty and lonely.

Those words do not give *any* justice to the way I felt at that time. Nor do those words give *any* justice to anyone who has thought about suicide or gone through with this action. I was on my knees and cocked the hammer back on the gun. For some unknown reason, I gave out one last prayer and asked God to *show* himself to me. I had nothing to live for at that time, so I thought. I put the gun into my mouth and had it in there for a while but could not work up my guts to pull the trigger. I laid the gun to my right side and went into the fetal position while on my knees. My right hand still held the pistol with the hammer cocked and my finger on the trigger.

As I laid my head down onto my left arm, the most wonderful feeling of peace came into that apartment. Following the feeling was a magnificent bright light. This light was so bright that I was squinting even with my eyes closed and my head into my arm. I don't know or remember how long this went on, but it was more than enough time to make me change my mind. I felt like if I moved, I would have been struck down right there. I *could not* move. I remember thinking, *I hope the air conditioning doesn't turn on,* because if even one hair on my head moved, I felt I would have died. It's a funny thing to say and ironic, when that was my goal anyway.

When I was able to finally get up off the floor, I was a brandnew person. All the depression, guilt, stress, and everything else that was on my shoulders left. At that point, I knew God had visited me in that room. My fire for God, needless to say, was kindled, like someone had just put a tank of gas and logs on a few coals. I didn't tell anyone of my experience for a little over a year. I went back to California to visit my aunt and uncle, who had continued to encourage me to the Lord and also to get re-baptized. After the baptism, they had a party for me to celebrate. My aunt and uncle and some of their friends were talking about being in the glory of God. As I listened to them, their experiences were close to mine. I got so excited that I forgot myself and interrupted them. I explained to them what had happened to me. At the conclusion of this conversation, I had found the truth of what happened to me. I was in the glory of God.

I have been trying to find some scripture to give folks an idea what God's glory is like. The Lord brought me to Exodus 33:19–23:

> And the Lord said, "I will cause all my goodness to pass in front of you, and I will proclaim my name, the Lord, in your presence. I will have mercy on whom I will have mercy, and I will have compassion on whom I will have compassion. But," he said, "you cannot see my face, for no one may see me and live." Then the Lord said, "There is a place near me where you may stand on a rock. When my glory passes by, I will put you in a cleft in the rock and cover you with my hand until I have passed by. Then I will remove my hand and you will see my back; but my face must not be seen."

I didn't get to see any part of the Lord, but his glory explained in this scripture was exactly what his glory felt like in that apartment that night. His glory and presence in that room felt like more than enough to kill me. I didn't need anything else to be sold out for God. Just a tip of his glory changed my life forever!

I was afraid if I had told anyone that they might send me to a loony bin. So, all in all, what happened to me with my ex-girlfriend came to a positive end to glorify God. I believe now that what I thought was love was actually more lust than anything. I regret a lot of my past, but I've been forgiven, and I praise God for that. I am very grateful for what she did. I hope her relationship with the Lord has grown as much as mine has. I want to say thank you to her for what she did. God used her to help me get back on his path.

When I wrote, "I couldn't take something that wasn't mine," I was bought at a price. The price was Jesus dying on the cross for my sins. My life was no longer mine as soon as I gave it to the Lord. Therefore, I couldn't take my life because it was not mine to take.

HEARD PRAYERS

When I pray for change,
That's invitation for my life to be rearranged.
Change is so very painful,
But in the end so very gainful.
As I get older,
I pray my fire not smolder.
Help me to be wiser.
With your word let me inspire.
May your way be known,
Many seeds sown.
The harvest is ripe.
Help shed light in peoples' night,
The end is near. Repent,
Or our good days, as we know them, will be spent.

For many years, the cry of my heart was that God would mold me and change my life so it would glorify him and the kingdom of heaven. What I didn't know at the time was that he would answer my prayers, but not in the way I hoped or had planned. Change brings a lot of pain, especially when we want God's will to be done in our lives. This is a time we give God permission to have his way. The pain comes when things don't happen in our timing or the way we think they should happen. This is the time we lose all fleshly rights and depend on the Spirit, rather than ourselves, to lead us. Some dreams we have will be cancelled, but most often, they get put into order—God's order.

As we walk in God's perfect will, he keeps us from traveling the wrong path and making mistakes we will later regret. This takes patience, something most people, including myself, don't have. During this time, he builds our foundation and character.

When I first asked Jesus to be my Savior, I wasn't ready to go and preach the Word. God is building my strength and character for me to do this later in my life. A house cannot stand in a flood if the foundation is made of paper-mâché. God does not do things prematurely. Our spiritual foundation needs to be deep and strong. That is exactly what God does to his servants—builds us up slowly and carefully. We will make mistakes, and he will discipline us, but only because he loves us. Don't rebuke the Lord's discipline; pray and ask him to give you insight. He will. You might not like it, but his way is the best way. Be still and at peace; God has plans for all our lives. Give him the time to build you up.

FREE GRACE

Hear God's grace,
For eternal life you will taste.
Do not be lazy,
Or let your vision be hazy.
Read God's Word with eagerness.
Leave behind all bitterness.
Let your heart not grow cold.
Preach God's Word and be bold.
Praise his holy name.
Do things not for fame.
Remember yourself last.
Forgive your past,
For God will remember no more
If you walk through his door.

Many people struggle with forgiving themselves of their past. I have struggled with this for years. This is an attack from the devil. If he can get our minds on something else or find a way to condemn us, he will use it. He wants to lure us off track so we will not fulfill God's will in our lives. Remember, conviction comes from the Lord, and condemnation comes from the devil. If we keep living in the would-have, could-have, and should-have mentality, we are missing the whole point of why Jesus died on the cross. He died on the cross to forgive our sins—our *past* sins and our *future* sins.

Not one of us will live a life like Jesus and not make mistakes. God knows when we sin, and the funny thing is, we know it too. You can't hide the sin from God, so why are you trying to hide it from yourself? Acknowledge that it is there and ask God to help you repent. Whether we want it to or not, our flesh will sneak in and we will sin. Don't let the devil have his way and condemn you for it; God doesn't. You can depend on God's grace and mercy. Do not abuse his mercy to the point that you keep satisfying your flesh and continue living in the sin because you know God will forgive you! Simply do the best you can do, and God will make up for what you are lacking. But this will take a lot of effort on your part. When God sees you try, that is when he will come in and make his presence known and open doors that only he can open and wants open.

GLORIFY

Smile for a while.
All problems to God are mild.
Be kind to a stranger.
Stay away from known danger.
God knows what it's like to be a man.
You were formed from his own hands.
Do not take away from the needy.
God's favor for them is speedy.
Take care of our own,
For our savior was born,
Jesus was lifted on high,
For it, he had to die.
We also must die to the flesh
Or life will be a mess.

I wrote this poem when it seemed as though God had forgotten all about me and the vows I had made to him. I didn't feel I was worthwhile or even had a part in his plan. I felt as if I were outside looking in at all the others doing things for the kingdom of heaven. The key words I used here are *feel* and *felt.* This is one of Satan's favorite tricks, using our emotions and feelings against us. We need to bind our minds to Christ Jesus and rebuke these emotions in his name. When we do this, these emotions have to flee far from us. It doesn't mean they will not be back; just keep rebuking them every time they try to sneak back in.

I was wallowing around, feeling sorry for myself, when in reality, God had been working overtime on me, preparing me for the work he has called me to do. A prayer we all need to pray is for God to prepare our hearts and minds for what he has already prepared for us before we were even a thought. Jack, a brother in Christ, told me to pray this.

The last part of this poem is something I am still going through and will for the rest of my life: dying to the flesh everyday. No matter how it looks, I believe every Christian struggles with this. From what I have witnessed, those who say they have control over every aspect of their lives seem to have the most struggles. We really want help, support, and prayer, but our pride steps in and says, "Oh, I'm fine. I don't need anything." Sound familiar? But Matthew 18:19 says, "Again, I tell you that if two of you on earth agree about *anything* you ask for, it will be done for you by my Father in heaven." So if this is what Jesus says to do, should you continue to fight your battle alone? Or should you come together and believe together to get quicker results?

Answered prayers will grow your faith in God. There is strength in numbers, and God will make sure you are not fighting your battles alone. Joining together with fellow believers will add to your support system by praying together through your battles.

FEAR NOT

Do not tremble,
For god's angels are assembled.
When under attack,
Take full authority, and give it back.
Do not give evil any room.
When Jesus comes, Satan will meet his doom.
Stay strong.
Do no wrong.
Do not stray from God's way,
Or you could pay in his day.
To fear the Lord is wisdom.
You will find favor in his kingdom.

Within two months, I had many attacks that could have taken my life. These attacks were in the form of car accidents. But I walked away with only a bump on my head and a scratch. The first two happened within ten minutes of each other; the second accident totaled the car. When the third and fourth accidents came a week later, I realized I was right in the middle of a spiritual war. Praise God, for he kept the passenger and me safe. This also excited me a little because I knew I was on the right path even though it didn't seem as if I was at the time. For my life was spared, and Satan will send out attacks once we choose to follow Christ.

Christians will go through attacks, whether it is on our lives, finances, family members, emotions, relationships, or anything the enemy can sink his claws into. He uses lust, unforgiveness, condemnation, feelings of unworthiness, and basically anything he can to dispose of God's children. Ephesians 6:12 says, "For our struggle is not against flesh and blood, but against the powers of this dark world and against the spiritual forces of evil in the heavenly realms."

I have learned from experience that we need to praise God in the good times and the bad. Most people forget to praise God during the good times because things are so easy, and claim it's too hard to praise him during the bad times. Praise is a must during both, especially during the bad.

Let's take fear and a horse for an analogy. If a horse has never been touched by human hands, it will fear you. You are considered a predator to that horse. To gain the horse's trust, we need to teach him that you are not a predator and that you do not want to harm him. To do this, you first put him in a round pen or a corral that is cozy, meaning not a lot of room, but enough room for him to do his dance. You will be close to the horse, and you will be invading his personal space. He will run, kick, and look for any way out. You need to be in the middle of that pen and give that horse plenty of space to run around you and do what he feels he needs to do. Amazingly enough, it does not take too long for that horse to start calming down and start getting curious about you.

See, you are a predator to that horse and predators attack and kill horses, but you're not attacking him. The horse's confusion will turn into curiosity, and he will start to communicate with you the only way he knows how, like a horse. He will lower his head while continuing to run from you. To a horse this is saying, "Okay, will you be my friend if you're not here to harm me?" In return, you say, "Yes, I do want to be your friend." You say this by easing off. By that I mean you lower your head, don't take steps toward him, and do not move suddenly. By taking steps toward him, you're saying that you are aggressive. By lowering your head and easing off, you in return are saying you no longer want to appear aggressive to him.

When he stops to check you out, you do these things.

You are teaching this horse not to fear you, just like God has been trying to teach us not to fear him or our circumstances. After all, are we not in his round pen? Has he not been trying to work with us? It only takes horses a few hours to get it, but for me it has taken years. I wish I was as smart as a horse.

When that horse starts lowering its head and

also starts licking its lips, you know he wants to be your friend. Now is the time to start building trust. Eventually he will come up to you. He will want to smell you and give you the low-down in a horse kind of way. Smelling you and watching your body language will tell that horse everything he needs to know about you.

See, body language is also important to us as humans, and it's all a part of communication. Once you and the horse have established some trust, it is time to start building some boundaries. If you do not want him to go on one side of the round pen, tell him. How? If he goes where you do not want him, let him know by whistling, waving a plastic bag, or clapping. Once he goes to the side you want him on, stop doing those things. He will learn fast that when he is over on the other side, he gets a lot of annoying noise that he does not like. But when he is on the side where there is no noise, he learns that he is in a safe place, which is what he wants. This is his reward for doing what you are telling him: peace and quiet.

So you are building trust and boundaries with him in his language—just like God is trying to do with us, day in and day out. Are you listening? Grant, a brother in Christ, helped sharpen my understanding on some of these points. Others have different ways to work with horses, this is just the way I like to work with them.

The first part of this poem is talking about not fearing the devil and his attacks. God's Holy Spirit and angels are assembled to protect us and guide us. But it is up to us to heed God's correction and his Word. Sometimes it seems like we can't handle what is thrown our way, but the Father doesn't give us things that we can't handle. Stay strong, praise God at all times, and fear the Lord. By doing these things, you can't go wrong.

PAID BY BLOOD

We were bought at a price.
Jesus' blood is precise.
He was born a man and died a king.
Therefore we should praise his name and sing.
Praise God, Jesus was obedient.
Glory to God for his lenience,
By faith, we receive our gift.
Always, his name we shall lift.
Let me not stray from God's way,
For I know the debt has been paid.
Salvation is what I preach.
By grace, this contract cannot be breached.
Praise the Lord,
For he did this on his own accord.

The more I realize what God did by sending his one and only Son Jesus to die for me, the more humbling it is. Could you send your only child away and let him suffer for things he didn't do? When we give our lives to Jesus, we are not our own anymore. First Corinthians 6:19–20 says, "You are not your own; you were bought at a price." He took all our sin—the past and future sin. That is a lot of sin that Jesus took upon himself. The blood of Jesus resembles the new covenant and cancels the old covenant. We do not have to sacrifice animals for their blood to be forgiven anymore like they did with the old covenant. If there was no shedding of blood, there was no forgiveness of sins.

Now we can just ask for forgiveness, and we have it. The old covenant required the sacrifice of animals, and through their blood, God forgave the sins of his people. Jesus ended that once and for all when he gave his life and his blood on the cross for any person *when* he or she accepts Jesus as his or her Lord and Savior. For he is the ultimate sacrifice, and no one and nothing else can bring the forgiveness of sins! Praise God!

Hebrews 9:11–28 explains all of this completely.

> When Christ came as high priest of the good things that are already here, he went through the greater and more perfect tabernacle that is not man-made, that is to say, not a part of this creation. He did not enter by means of the blood of goats and calves; but he entered the Most Holy Place once for all by his own blood, having obtained eternal redemption. The blood of goats and bulls and the ashes of a heifer sprinkled on those who are ceremo-

nially unclean sanctify them so that they are outwardly clean. How much more, then, will the blood of Christ, who through the eternal Spirit offered himself unblemished to God, cleanse our consciences from acts that lead to death, so that we may serve the living God!

For this reason Christ is the mediator of a new covenant, that those who are called may receive the promised eternal inheritance-now that he has died as a ransom to set them free from the sins committed under the first covenant.

In the case of a will, it is necessary to prove the death of the one who made it, because a will is in force only when somebody has died; it never takes effect while the one who made it is living. This is why even the first covenant was not put into effect without blood. When Moses had proclaimed every commandment of the law to all the people, he took the blood of calves, together with water, scarlet wool and branches of hyssop, and sprinkled the scroll and all the people. He said, "This is the blood of the covenant, which God has commanded you to keep." In the same way, he sprinkled with the blood both the tabernacle and everything used in its ceremonies. In fact, the law requires that nearly everything be cleansed with blood, and without the shedding of blood there is *no* forgiveness.

It was necessary, then, for the copies of the heavenly things to be purified with these sacrifices, but the heavenly things themselves

> with better sacrifices than these. For Christ did not enter a man-made sanctuary that was only a copy of the true one; he entered heaven itself, now to appear for us in God's presence. Nor did he enter heaven to offer himself again and again, the way the high priest enters the Most Holy Place every year with blood that is not his own. Then Christ would have had to suffer many times since the creation of the world. But now he has appeared once and for all at the end of the ages to do away with sin by the sacrifice of himself. Just as man is destined to die once, and after that to face judgment, so Christ was sacrificed once to take away the sins of many people; and he will appear a second time, not to bear sin, but to bring salvation to those who are waiting for him.

Praise God that he does not hold us to the old covenant anymore. The old covenant pretty much went according to our works. It is so simple now through the blood of Jesus. But remember, there is an enemy that prowls around like a lion seeking anyone he can devour. Satan knows the Word of God very well and has manipulated God's Word very well to mislead many into his own plan. He is not to be tolerated, but respected. Jesus has won! Satan has to flee far from you when you tell him to in Jesus' name!

Now let's go to Revelation 22:13. "I am the Alpha and the Omega, the First and the Last, the Beginning and the End." This verse is saying that Jesus is the only way. He is the now and later, the is and the is to be, the first to die and be raised from the dead and the last and only one that can save us. He is the only way to the Father. If you are trying to get to heaven any other way, I'm afraid I have some bad news for you: The heaven you are working your way toward will be a little hot!

STYLED TRIALS

During your trial,
God watches how you keep your style.
Try not to doubt,
Or even try a different route.
Be quiet and still.
No matter how steep the hill,
When the time is right,
God will show you his guiding light.

As we face trials every day, our Father watches us. He knows what we think and how we feel. He watches how you handle what is given to you.

Let's take finances, for instance. Are you praying for extra money to come in? The Father will watch if you tithe or give offerings. Remember, when you're faithful in the little, you will also be faithful in the big. If you're not being faithful with what you have now, should God bless you more? Would you bless your children with more freedom or finances if they were running crazy and spent all of their allowance on bubble gum? I don't believe so. Should God bless you more if you are running crazy and not being faithful with what you have? I don't believe he should, but that, of course, is my opinion!

Doubt comes to every believer. Having faith is sure to bring attacks from the enemy. Deep down inside, we all have a little doubt. You could be thinking, *I don't deserve this kind of blessing,* or, *No way would God bless me that much.* That is not what God says in the Holy Bible, unless I'm reading a different Bible than you. The one that I read says he wants to bless me, not just to bless me, but for me to go out and bless others as well. But also go with that gut instinct that is called the Holy Spirit as well. Blessings should not stop with us. They should carry on to others. We know what the Word says, but do we apply it?

Don't go out and try to take a different route. This is usually when we prolong our wait and our struggles. Be still and try to wait patiently, even when it seems to take forever. When God sees you being faithful in what you have and faithful in the tasks he has given you now, he will give you more. But remember, his time is the best time. We usually want things prematurely. God needs to prepare us for what he has planned for us. So what kind of attitude are you going to have during your trial? It is, after all, your choice.

TO RECEIVE

Please, God, use me today.
Show me your will and way.
Help me witness to a nonbeliever.
Let their spirit be a receiver.
Lord, speak through me,
So they may see
The grace you give,
So eternal life they may live.

If Christians have a defect, it would be not witnessing enough, in my opinion. We fear what people will think, and we do not want to lose friendships. But what kind of friendship or love do we have if we don't witness to them? Can you handle it if one of your family members dies and hasn't accepted Jesus as their Lord and Savior, and you didn't say anything to them?

The Father will give us the words to say, but we also need to start saying something for him to deliver. Don't meditate and think your way out of witnessing. If you think too much, then you tend to be afraid of what you will say. When you witness from your heart, God will give the words you need because that is where God is living—in your heart. Keep it simple. Tell them how you accepted Jesus as your Lord and Savior; share your testimony! Tell them that Jesus is the only begotten Son of God and he died on the cross for all people's sin, including theirs, rose from the dead three days later, and now sits at the right hand of God in the kingdom of heaven. By sacrificing his body and giving his blood, Jesus, the only one without sin, took on the world's sin so we could be forgiven if we choose to believe by *faith* what he did was for us.

Pray! The Father will give you the right words that need to be spoken. God is faithful and will do it. We just need to be faithful and give him something to work with.

THE HOST

I pray for the host,
The Holy Ghost.
To this guy I make the most.
For he helps my day coast
Guide me, lead me, and show me.
Open the eyes of my heart, for this is your key.
I only pray that people will see
That your grace now is free.

We always try to do things by ourselves. This is where we usually end up wanting to eat our words or stick our heads in sand, doing the ostrich stance.

Before we witness, we need to pray and ask the Holy Spirit to be present. Most times, you have no idea an opportunity to witness is coming. Arm yourself with God's Word at all times. Deep in your heart, you can cry out for help, and the Father will sound the charge bugle for his angels to show and his Holy Spirit to work through you. After all, you're witnessing to bring a soul into his kingdom. He will come in force for your support. Whenever your heart's desire is to do his will, he will come in more ways than you have ever dreamed of.

God does care how we promote his name and his kingdom. After all, your reputation is no longer just yours, but the one you are promoting: *God!*

SHARED TESTIMONY

If you're a believer,
Of eternal life you're a receiver.
This gift, do not hide.
Salvation to the lost should not be denied.
It's up to you
To get through.
Use the Bible to give the clues,
And your testimony too.
Pour out your heart.
The rest is God's part.
Share about your salvation.
Winning souls for heaven is retaliation.
Whatever you do, don't stop.
Then the devil's plans will flop.

What would happen if you were out in the forest and came upon a creek and something was glistening in the water? As you came up closer to investigate, you realize that it was gold! What would you do? Would you run back to your friends and tell them all about it and then give them a map? I'll bet your answer is, "No way." The things that would run through your mind would be to keep quiet, go back and get supplies, and get someone whom you can trust to help get it out.

Is this greediness? Don't get me wrong; I'd be ahead of you to do the same thing, but this is how a lot of Christians treat their salvation, in a way of speaking. This treasure needs to be shared, for nothing in this world is your own; it's God's.

Many of us leave witnessing up to pastors or evangelists or someone else that we *feel* God has anointed for that job. Do you say to yourself, "I sure hope a pastor comes to each one of my family members' doors and leads them to their salvation"? Does that sound stupid? Well, it's not just up to the "holy people," it's up to you and me and anyone who has his or her salvation.

You don't need to be a preacher to lead people to Christ, just like it doesn't take a farmer to plant seeds for every plant in the world. It is God's job to plant the forests and jungles. God uses the wind to scatter the seed, water to nourish, and soil for it to grow. Just as the Father uses us to scatter seeds, then it is his job to water and encourage those seeds to grow along with our help wherever and whenever it's needed. Do your best, and God will work with what you plant. Use your testimony and the Bible; you will not go wrong. Never stop planting seeds. We already know God has won eternally, but the fight is now for every soul. God needs your help, and you need his! Don't hide this treasure, for treasure greater than gold waits for you in heaven!

REMEMBER SEPTEMBER

Soldiers they were not,
But died as if they fought.
America, repent from your sins,
Or our future will be dim.
Freedom costs lives.
Quit living American lies.
Life has been lost,
Including our Savior's on the cross.
What a gift God gave us.
But we chase wealth and lust.
America, America, repent.
God has blessed us.
Now, America, bless God …
Remember September!

We will never forget that day in September 2001. The thousands of people who lost their lives that day in the twin towers were not soldiers, but died as if they were in uniform and in the middle of a war. They were in a war, but one we could not see or hear coming—a spiritual war. When I speak of America needing to repent from sins, that is exactly what I mean. So many Americans are turning from God and his ways and turning to other so-called gods, such as money, drugs, sex, so-called *spiritual journeys,* stealing, murder, and divorce. There are many other sins we need to repent of also; these are just a few.

If we look back in the Old Testament and the New Testament, we will see how God has blessed cities, countries, lands, and his people. But we also will see his people stray from his ways and go their own direction. God sends his prophets and warnings so many times to tell us to turn from our ways and get back on track with his ways.

In the Old Testament, they killed his prophets and ignored his warnings. Nothing has changed today. We still ignore his warnings and still kill his prophets. It seems as if we do not want to believe what we see or hear, but how can we not believe what we see and hear? That is how most people believe in things anyway. Not too many people seem to have faith these days. The end days are here, folks, and we should not ignore the warnings any longer!

So what did God do then? What should he do now? In the Old Testament, he took his blessings away from his people and let them go their own way. Whatever evil their hearts were desiring, God fulfilled and made their hearts burn even more with that kind of evil. Their lands were scorched and dried up and stopped producing food and water and basically laid barren to this day. Should we take some of the things we see today as a warning? I do. I pray for protection and continued blessings, and I repent of my sins to the best of my ability, which is not perfect. I can't repent for your sins or the world's, but we can repent of our own. Our spiritual freedom was bought at a price—Jesus dying on the cross.

God has blessed this nation beyond any other nation. But many of us do not appreciate it, and we just want more. Do not let the death of Jesus or our soldiers be done in vain. For if it weren't for their sacrifices, we wouldn't have eternal life and our freedom we enjoy! If you have food and shelter, then you have more than the majority of people in many nations. But we as Americans keep chasing more and more; we can never get enough, it seems.

Money, power, and lust have been running this country for some time. Look at what an ex-president did, having oral sex and basically, committing adultery, then getting off scot-free. Soldiers are court marshaled. What is good for the goose is good for the gander; isn't that how the saying goes? Government leadership put these kinds of rules on civilians; they need to abide by them as well. Letting him off sent a huge message to me and should have spoken to other adults about where morals are going in this country. The administration needed a head check as much as that president did.

People are being inspired by their five senses—what feels good, what tastes good, what smells good, what sounds good, and what looks good. The sad thing is that people are trying to fill a void they feel in their lives. But filling this void with sin is only buying them a one-way ticket to hell. Brothers and sisters, God has blessed us! Now let's bless God and get back on his track. His blessings will return even more than ever.

God bless you soldiers that have fought for my freedom and ones that died on that September day! I will not let my Savior's death or the ones that have died to keep me free be done in vain! *Remember September!*

LEFT ALONE

God, why have you left?
Has my heart grown deaf?
I feel the effects of the battle,
Like I'm going upstream with out a paddle.
Help me keep praise in my mouth.
Let your peace rest on this house.
I was once so strong.
From my spirit sang an awesome song.
Return your peace.
Let it not cease,
For somehow I've found trouble.
Please bring back your presence on the double!

When I wrote this poem, I felt as if the Lord left my side. I wondered if my heart had grown cold or deaf to the Spirit of God. Some battles for Christians are tough and unbearable. It felt as if I was in the boxing ring with the heavyweight champion of the world and handcuffed.

Sometimes it feels like we don't want to go on. But then somewhere comes strength. Praise God! He gives us all that we need, when we need it. Psalm 68:35 says, "You are awesome, O God, in your sanctuary; the God of Israel gives power and strength to his people." We all know or can imagine what it would feel like trying to go upstream without a paddle. Sometimes that's exactly how it feels going through spiritual battles. Even though we all go through battles, I pray that we all keep praise on our lips, for God is good, and in his time he will deliver us out of our hard times.

When we continue to praise God during the hard times, we are passing a major test, and we also are rebuking the devil. God will call off the battles in time, but we must not give up on him. The Lord will give us many tests to see how we will react; that is the time to stay strong. The only way to lose our battles is giving up.

Galatians 6:9 says, "Let us not become weary in doing good, for at the proper time we will reap a harvest if we do not give up." In due time, all things come together for the good and for your best interest. Pray that his peace will reign over your life. This is easier said than done sometimes, I know, but he will give you the strength you need. Sometimes it seems we can just not escape trouble. Just continue to praise God's name, for who he is and what he does. The secret to winning your battles is *praise!*

PRAYED DREAMS

Sometimes sleep
is my mind's only time of peace.
I don't feel the hurt or confusion.
Life then isn't an illusion.
I can't feel my loneliness.
I can't think of my holiness.
Time is only on God's side;
all I can do is go along for the ride.
So, God, when I sleep,
I pray it's sweet and deep.
Life isn't peaches and cream,
So, Lord, when I sleep, bring a peaceful dream.

For the last eight years, it seemed the only peace I had was when I slept. I hoped and prayed I'd dream peaceful dreams. When I slept, I couldn't feel any pain, stress, confusion, or loneliness. I don't live in the flesh when I sleep. Meaning, I don't have bad thoughts or any temptations running over my mind every other second. Some dreams are not from God, and the devil does bring nightmares.

"I can't think of my own holiness" means that whenever I'm awake, I'm constantly wondering if what I'm doing is glorifying God or myself. This isn't bad, but it does get tiring.

As humans, we don't have much time on our hands. We are only here for a short while, and we are judged on what we *believe* in our hearts and what we *do* in that short period of time. God has all the time in the world to do what he wants. We don't. We might be here, on average, seventy years. He will use us if we will let him and we should be prepared to hang on tight once we decide to take the ride on his path for us.

If you choose your own path, then you are denying God's path. So will your way still have the same blessings and eternal outcome? It may seem to be fun and games here on earth, but will you think that when it is your time to be judged? This poem is a little depressing, I know, but this is how I feel sometimes, and I believe a lot of others do also. Living here on earth is hard at times and tiring, but God does give his children rest. Isaiah 32:18 says "My people will live in peaceful dwelling places, in secure homes, in undisturbed places of rest." But I do know one thing: God loves all of us very much, and I can't imagine how his heart breaks every time ours do. I also know that he will turn things around to benefit himself, and us, but only in his time.

If you think about it for a minute, earth is the only hell you and I will ever know if you know Jesus as your Lord and Savior. If you don't know him as your Lord and Savior, then life here on earth could be the only piece of heaven you will ever know.

Sometimes life doesn't deal us good cards; I couldn't even try to imagine what hell would be like for eternity. Do not let this free gift of salvation pass you up. You just need to drop your pride and quit trying to make sense of everything. You will never know everything, and if you wait too long, it will be too late, for death will find us all. You have to find salvation before your time is up; it could be tomorrow or fifty years from now. Isaiah 56:1 hints toward this statement, "Maintain justice and do what is right, for my salvation is close at hand and my righteousness will soon be revealed." So we have no idea when our time is at hand. We better be prepared now. Are you willing to gamble with your only soul and the only chance to be saved? I hope not! If you are a gambler, then sleep may be the only peace you will ever know or experience. I pray that you don't take that risk, waiting until later, because that later could become now. Sleep tight!

SCHOOL FOR SCHOLARS

On God's path I strolled,
Holy spirit school, I enrolled.
The Holy Bible is the only book to buy for this class.
It teaches principles that will last.
Many are out to deceive.
In Jesus' name, do not receive.
Command that spirit to leave.
Truth only comes through Jesus, the
only one you can believe!

Once, I thought I was on God's path and that I was doing fine. That was also the time in my life that I lived to please my flesh. Then Jesus really came into my life, and I realized that my flesh was telling me I was doing fine, but my soul was in trouble.

Everyday, I realize more and more what a sinner I still am, even after I have accepted Jesus as my Lord and Savior. We are all still sinners, but Jesus died on the cross for all sin, not just sin you committed before Jesus was your Savior. He died for the continuous sins we commit. We will continue to make mistakes, and God knows it. He forgives and has forgiven. But we need to quit using God's grace like we use toilet paper. God does *not* condemn, but he does *convict* you of your sin. John 16:8 backs this up, "When he comes, he will convict the world of guilt in regard to sin and righteousness and judgment in regard to sin, because men do not believe in me." Let's get real! We all know when we are living in sin without the conviction. Acknowledge it, ask for forgiveness, and move on. Quit using God's grace like you just stepped out of a public restroom!

Enroll in Holy Spirit school. God will let you take his classes. They are free. You can get all you ever need to know out of the Bible, and the Holy Spirit will direct you rest of the way. The Bible and Jesus Christ are the *only* ones we can trust. There are many religions that claim they have the truth, but in reality the enemy will camouflage the truth for lies and deceptive theories. What sounds intriguing to a person is usually what the enemy will use to deceive a person. So we basically set ourselves up.

Romans 10:9–10 says, "That if you confess with your

mouth, 'Jesus is Lord,' and believe in your heart that God raised him from the dead, you *will* be saved. For it is with your heart that you believe and are justified, and it is with your mouth that you confess and are saved." That is all it takes to get into heaven. Not by works alone, but by what you believe in your heart!

Ephesians 2:8–9 says, "For it is by grace you have been saved; through faith—and this not from yourselves, it is the gift of God—not by works; so that no one can boast." So, if a religion says you are saved by the things you do and say … we *all* would be in deep trouble. Our works cannot save us; it is what you believe in your heart by faith that will save you, but we are judged on our works and rewards will be determined on judgment day. Matthew 16:27 says, "For the Son of Man is going to come in his Fathers glory with his angels, and then he will reward each person according to what he has done." If works saved us, we all would think we were better than everyone else, as it is stated in the scripture I just wrote, "so that no one can boast."

Or what about the religion that says not to step on bugs or kill animals, because it could be one of your ancestors? Wow! They wouldn't like me. Thank God that isn't true; I wouldn't have a family tree.

The point is, the list goes on and on. The only way to save souls is to witness. Speak what is truth and what is just and live what you preach, or as close as you can. For many will call you a hypocrite if you do something wrong, and they are no better for judging you when their actions are no better or worse. Many with deep convictions sometimes tend to project their guilt onto someone else.

I'm not bashing other religions, but I pray that God

will show followers of false doctrine the truth. Religions that preach false doctrines have millions of believers. We need to be on our knees and pray for these people and also pray that we are not deceived in the process. Times are short, people. Bible prophecy is passing us by everyday.

TODAY'S TOMORROW

Lord, today help me plant a seed.
To your instruction, help me heed.
Give me hunger for your Word to read.
Please exterminate in me any weeds.
Guide me and show me by your lead.
Help me walk upright in my deeds
And fulfill all your needs.
Lord, tomorrow help me plant a seed.

Is this the kind of prayer that you pray everyday? If not, it's a good one to start praying. We could change peoples' lives with one simple, "God bless you" or "Jesus loves you."

Have you ever prayed, "Please, God, if you are real, do this"? I'll bet most people can say yes to this question. Well, if you have prayed for something like this, don't you think others do the same? So one simple "God bless you" could answer a prayer and encourage a lost soul. One simple act of love could make or take a soul into heaven or hell.

Do not be shy! I know it's easier said than done sometimes. It will take you time to figure out your style of witnessing. Your style will not be the same as any other style. But God will bring out your character and style if you ask him to. I've come to realize the hard way that if we put ourselves last and serve others first, God will bless us in many ways. He also sees to it that we have whatever we ask for as long as it is his will.

Whatever you do and wherever you go today or tomorrow, plant eternal seeds!

DETOUR AHEAD

Protect your thoughts,
For a great battle is being fought.
God will send us aid.
Resist the devil's raids.
He will put evil into your mind.
In Jesus' name, rebuke and bind.
If your thinking begins to stink,
The devil's attacks, you can link.
Your mind is his playground.
But rest assured, for eternal life you found.
Satan is here to kill, steal, and destroy.
In the end, his attacks were just a decoy.

If you know Jesus as your Lord and Savior, then Satan's attacks are just a decoy. If you don't know Jesus as Lord and Savior, then his attacks are for his own glory, winning your soul for his kingdom in hell.

Our minds and our emotions are where the devil uses strategy for his attacks. He uses doubt, insecurity, depression, stress, anxiety, jealousy, hate, and anger, to name a few. Have you ever experienced any of these emotions or attacks? Everyone has at one point or another. Second Peter 5:8–9 says,

> "Be self-controlled and alert. Your enemy the devil prowls around like a roaring lion looking for someone to devour. Resist him, standing firm in the faith, because you know that your brothers throughout the world are undergoing the same kind of sufferings."

Every single person that knows Jesus Christ as their personal Savior *will* experience attacks. The Bible tells us this, but in so many cases, we *feel* as if we are the only ones having problems. This is a decoy that the devil is sending out. If you are worried about your physical or financial or emotional problems, then you are not going out winning souls or doing God's will. I'm as guilty of this as anyone.

Second Peter 5:8–9 is telling us to resist him. You can do it! Satan is just messing with your head! What is the first thing you think about when you wake up in the morning? Is it your problems? Or how you can witness to someone today? If the devil can engulf us in our problems, then he doesn't have to worry about us doing God's will.

This is a constant battle, day in and day out. The way to control and win this constant battle is reforming and renewing your minds to Christ Jesus. Romans 12:2 states, "Do not conform any longer to the pattern of this world, but be transformed by the renewing of your mind. Then you will be able to test and approve what God's will is—his good, pleasing and perfect will."

Reforming and renewing your mind is easier said than done. Unfortunately, many people don't know how. The step is pretty simple. When your mind wanders off, thinking about worldly sin, the trick is *do not entertain those thoughts and renew your mind by reading the Bible.*

But sometimes we just dive right on in, and before we know it, we have a full motion picture going on in our minds. Every time adultery, idolatry, hate, or any evil thoughts come into your mind, stop entertaining them and transform those thoughts to God and his will and again renew your mind with God's Word.

Pray that God will give you discernment and wake you up from entertaining those evil thoughts. It is simple in theory, but hard in reality. With the help of the Father, it can be done. First John 4:4 says, "You, dear children, are from God and have overcome them, because the one who is in you is greater than the one who is in the world." Remember Luke 1:37: "For nothing is impossible with God."

We can stand on these promises. If we couldn't stand on these promises, that would make God a liar, and we know he can't lie. Hebrews 6:18 backs this up: "God did this so that, by two unchangeable things in which it is impossible for God to lie, we who have fled to take hold of the hope offered to us may be greatly encouraged." So be encouraged and stand firm. God is here and knows your problems and your heart, and he will give you your heart's desires if you do not give up.

PAID IN FULL

Set your mind on the cross,
For Jesus paid the cost,
So none would be lost.
These were orders from the boss.
Pray that God burns out our dross.
In time, the devil to hell will be tossed.

Set your mind on Jesus and what he did for the world. Pray so you won't be deceived. These days, the average life to be lived is around seventy years, give or take. It is what we *believe* in that period of time that will determine where we go for eternity. Live life everyday like it is your last here on earth.

How many times have we heard words like the ones I write? Repetition seems to be the only way we learn. How many times did our parents have to repeat themselves to get us to do things? For my parents, it seemed the average was at least three times. Then, the last time, they were good and mad and started yelling or paddling; then it finally sunk in.

God repeats himself and gives more warnings than any parent I know. It is hard to believe that we need so many reminders. This doesn't apply to everyone, but the majority. It is said many times in the Bible that we will reap what we sow. Make sure what you sow glorifies the Father and the kingdom of heaven. Ask God to burn the impurities out of your heart so your prayers will not be hindered.

We all know what is going to happen when the time draws to an end. We know what the future holds for Satan and his followers. But the battle now is for every soul here on earth. Get out there and bless someone, encourage someone, and most of all, witness to him or her. Seek the Lord's way to witness. He will open a door.

If you do not know Jesus as your Lord and Savior, your time is short. Get in touch with someone who will lead you in a prayer to ask Jesus into your heart. If you say a prayer just to say it, I do not believe you're accomplishing much. It needs to be in your heart. You need to want to know Jesus as your Lord and Savior and want to follow his ways and repent from your sin. Do not be ashamed to tell people that you are a Christian. Tell them and witness to them.

An empty prayer is a prayer in vain.

DELAY FOREPLAY

Sex before marriage
Could get you pregnant or result in a miscarriage.
It might give you a disease incurable,
One causing pain and suffering that's unbearable.
The ones spreading it don't give a rip.
You do not want to take that kind of trip.
Consequences you might think unreasonable,
The cost of medicine unfeasible.
Stay pure,
For your protection is sure.
If you burn with desire,
Pray for Holy Spirit fire.
Save the foreplay
For another day.
Wait for your spouse
In your own house.

Sex outside of marriage has been a problem since the time Adam and Eve were deceived. If you can't control your hormones, pray and ask the Lord to help you out. While you're at it, go take a cold shower when you feel that urge to splurge. That cold shower will give the Lord something to work with.

Some people sleep more in other people's beds than in their own. Many of them get girls pregnant and also spread sexual diseases. For some, the solution for pregnancy is abortion. The solution for diseases is to ignore them and give them to others.

Many with diseases couldn't care less if you get what they have. They go out and sleep with others, spreading what someone else gave them. They are merely thinking of five minutes of pleasure for themselves that will affect you for the rest of your life. I know how hard it is to control yourself, and you cannot do it without the Lord. I too, when younger, slept around. But not anymore; I've repented. With God's strength, I have been able to stay pure since I've asked Jesus into my heart. Not by my strength, but by the Father's, was I able to do this.

I now wait for the Lord to show me my wife. He will give you the strength and willpower, but you have to apply it. The best thing you can do for yourself is not put yourself in a position where you will be tempted. The Holy Spirit will give you the power to escape those emotions. But the true test is yours. God will do his part; but you must do your part. Remember, leave room for the Holy Ghost. Attraction is good, but do not let that attraction turn into lust, which will turn into sin. The only way to assure your protection and a clear conscience is to make up your mind that you will not kiss or even hold someone if you can't deal with the emotions. It might sound extreme, but this is what I had to do. We are still human, and if you give a millimeter to the devil, he will take a mile and send an all-out offense to get you to glorify him and his kingdom of hell. First Corinthians 6:18 says, "Flee from sexual immorality. All other sins a man commits are outside his body, but he who sins sexually sins against his own body. Do you not know that your body is a temple of the Holy Spirit, who is in you, whom you have received from God? You are not your own; you were bought at a price. Therefore honor God with your body."

A BULL RIDER'S PRAYER

As I live the cowboy way,
Protection is what I pray.
I don't know my fate
Outside of the gate.
If my ride sees trouble,
Send angels on the double.
For in you, Lord, I rest.
Let my life pass your test.
By pure grace I'm saved.
Lord, ride with me, for your way is paved.
That's the cowboy way
And what bull riders pray!

In my younger and dumber days, I used to ride bulls and bareback horses in rodeos. I started at the local rodeo in my hometown and then proceeded to ride in college. My best event was bareback horses. I even went professional for a couple of years and then decided I'd better leave it up to the true professionals. My time in the rodeos were some of the best times in my life and some of the most painful. I loved it, though, and I still do. At the end of my life, I won't regret not trying everything I wanted to. I tried, realized that rodeo was not my calling, and moved on.

During this time in my life was when my relationship started with God. This poem is a simple type of prayer that almost every cowboy says in one way or another. We all prayed in our own special way, and I would be hard-pressed to believe any cowboy who says they don't pray. I know the good Lord saved my bacon a few times. Each and every time that chute gate opened, there was a chance I could die or be seriously hurt. If and when trouble came, my prayer would be for me to be able to stay on my feet and get my hand out of my bareback rigging or bull rope.

If you ride with your right hand, you need to jump off or get off on the right side. If you get bucked off on the left, your hand will more than likely hang up in that rope or rigging. If that happens, you're in for a longer ride than eight seconds and could end up with a long stay at the local hospital.

Rodeo taught me a lot of what I needed in life, discipline being one of the major ones. I wrote a slogan that wraps up accomplishing your dreams: "Your discipline must be greater than the passion of your dreams." You can have all the passion in the world, but without the discipline, that passion is just passion. 2 Timothy 1:7 says, "For God did not give us a spirit of timidity, but a spirit of power, of love and of self-discipline." Success takes discipline; without discipline, you will not succeed! I also realized my discipline in rodeo was not like that of a world champion.

Nevertheless, the Lord was leading my discipline toward what he wanted me to do—his will. Rodeos were not his will, but he let me dibble dabble in it for a while until it was time for me to grow up. Don't get me wrong. This was not my calling, but it is the calling of many other great cowboys. Cowboys don't get paid unless they ride and win. It's not like we got paid when we had a sprained pinky like a lot of professional sports. This was also a part of discipline; how hurt was I? If I don't ride and win, I'm not going to have gas money to get home.

So riding became more of a job than fun. To become a world champion in any sport, it will take discipline. Champions don't sit on the couch asking God to drop it in their lap. They go out and give something God can work with. If you don't have the discipline to accomplish your dreams, then what makes you think you will have the discipline for the responsibilities that will follow the success of those dreams?

UNCONDITIONAL

Conviction brings bad moods.
To loved ones we tend to be rude.
At these times, it's better to keep our mouths shut,
Until God brings us out of that rut.
Heed God's conviction.
Put Satan on restriction.
No matter what, show love.
This recipe will fit like a glove.
Remember the ones that are close,
For they love you the most.
They are the ones that will see you through,
So stick to them like glue.

Trials and convictions seem to bring a lot of moodiness. This is what I have experienced during my trials. Sometimes when I have been convicted, it didn't matter what my loved ones said. I just tended to let them have a piece of my mind, even when I knew I was wrong. My parents always said, "If you can't say anything nice, then don't say anything at all." Ever hear that? 2 Thessalonians 1:4–5 says, "Therefore, among God's churches we boast about your perseverance and faith in all the persecutions and trials you are enduring. All this is evidence that God's judgment is right, and as a result you will be counted worthy of the kingdom of God, for which you are suffering." See, this one verse states we will have trials, but it also states during your trials you need to have perseverance, and stick to it until you get victory. No victory is given to those who quit.

Let God do his work and pray about what needs to be done in your circumstances. A lot of times, God will speak through your loved ones, trying to get something across to you. Heed his conviction; listen to others, for God might be speaking through them. But then again, he may not be either. Godly advice is not a bash fest, meaning that if you're getting sound advice, it usually will not end up ripping a person to shreds on their wrongs. Instead, it will help you discern some solutions to problems, not making the problem bigger or more out of hand in your mind. Wise council will listen to both sides before giving advice. Ignorance will only listen and believe one side.

God is not condemning you by telling you to quit doing what you're doing. But he does want you to repent. Isaiah 30:15 says this about repentance, "This is what the sovereign Lord, the Holy One of Israel, says: "In repentance and rest is your salvation, in quietness and trust is your strength, but you would have none of it." Verses 16–18 talk about how some flee on horses, and quit, but the Lord does not want us to quit, he wants us to continue and he will show graciousness and compassion for those who wait for him. Look it up, it is interesting. So when we repent he gives us rest, strength, graciousness and compassion. So maybe we should do the same for loved ones who are only trying their best to be there for you.

Moodiness comes when God is telling you to quit doing what you're doing and repent. But don't bite people's heads off, because ones who truly love you are the only ones that will be there for you and help you through whatever you're going through. Take the full authority that God gave you, and kick the devil of moodiness out and back to where he belongs. Treat others the way you want to be treated, remember that?

So remember, your family and ones who truly love you want to help you through whatever you are going through and help you find solutions, not more problems. Yes, sometimes they get annoying and on the nerves, but love them and thank them, and if you feel like ripping their heads off, let them know you love them and appreciate what they are trying to do. Then kick them out of your house or room. Just kidding. But try to be politically correct when asking for your space.

HOPEFUL TRUTH

In the truth, I put my hope.
Without it, I couldn't cope.
We all share a fate,
One that we all can relate:
The physical death,
When our bodies let out our last breath.
God's salvation, I praise,
For my spirit will raise.
I will suffer no more.
Where there is neither rich nor poor,
The Father I will worship.
We'll come together in courtship.

Can you imagine living without God's promises and not having the gift of salvation? I can't now, but years ago, when I didn't know Jesus as my Lord and Savior, I didn't care or wasn't interested in the truth. I thought God and I were just fine with the way things were. But living the way I was living was far from being okay with God. I went to church a few times when I was younger and got the basics of religion. But the "religious traditions" were not the entire truth; it was simply the basics of the truth. Mark 7:9 says this, "And he said to them: "You have a fine way of setting aside the commands of God in order to observe your own traditions." I feel that I got the traditions, such as communion, but never was I asked if I wanted to have a personal relationship with Jesus.

When you get into a full- blown relationship with Jesus, everything you thought you knew about religion goes right down the drain. He is alive, and God does as much now as he did back in Moses' day. But people ignore God's signs and turn away from hearing his faint whisper and applying his principles. You know when God has touched you because everything about him is alive. The feelings, the Bible, and your salvation are alive. It is nothing but pure joy when the blindfold is removed from your eyes. You can't help but share what you have found.

But sometimes people just don't share the same enthusiasm. One thing that all people have in common is death. We all experience the physical death. The second death for some is when they are condemned to hell for eternity. The righteous, on the other hand, will receive their gift of eternal life in the kingdom of heaven with the Father and the Son. Those who accept

Jesus by *faith* will have this great joy on that great day! For others, there will be great pain and sorrow. Revelation 21:6–8 says,

> He said to me: "It is done. I am the Alpha and the Omega, the Beginning and the End. To him who is thirsty I will give to drink without cost from the spring of the water of life. He who overcomes will inherit all this, and I will be his God and he will be my son. But the cowardly, the unbelieving, the vile, the murderers, the sexually immoral, those who practice magic arts, the idolaters and all liars—their place will be in the fiery lake of burning sulfur. This is the second death."

Praise his name, believers, because after leaving the tent of our bodies, we will be in the Father's glory. No more sickness, no rich or poor, no more hate, and so much more. For the ones who do not know Jesus as Lord and Savior, ask him into your heart! Believers will come together in his court and have true everlasting fellowship with the Almighty, the one and only God the Father.

REMEMBERED VOWS

We have so many dates,
Praying for the Lord to bring us our mates.
We finally meet the one and think, *Wow!*
In a few months, we exchange vows.
Children come along.
Before we know it, we're a dad and mom.
We find out love's real meaning.
As proud parents, we're gleaming.
Remember these feelings,
For in troubled times, they will bring healing.

When looking for our spouse, we have many dates seeking that right one. When we're ready for marriage, we are hopeful on every date that this could be it. I believe the good Lord will have to whack me over the head with a two-by-four or have her run me over with a Hummer for me to realize she is here, so it seems. Well, neither one has happened yet! Heck, I would settle for a VW bug as well.

Asking for strength, patience, and understanding is essential. I only speak of what I have noticed in successful marriages. When two people come together as one, you will have differences, and many times in the beginning, those differences are what attract you to the other person. Don't go into a relationship thinking you can change that person because you will have a bear that seemed to have been robbed of her cubs on your hands. But also understand this: You are no longer your own, but also your partner's.

Partners might like you to do something you do not like or are not used to, but humor them; do it. The only way to stay strong is to keep one another happy, and you always want favor with your spouse. So don't be stubborn; give in a little. It won't kill you, but just might bring more sparks into your love life. I'm sure we all can agree that there is nothing wrong with that.

In the hard times, remember why you married that person in the first place. Think of all the good times and not the few bad times. Remember, too, that Satan is after everyone he can get his slimy paws on. He will try to come between marriages any way he can. Do not let him in, or win. You need to come together with your spouse. If you're the man of the house and read the Bible, then you know it's your job to be the head of the house. In filling that role, remember to love your wife and listen to her opinions before you make the final decisions. Your wife will bring different views on the subject and help you to make a wiser decision. Ephesians 5:22–24 says for the wives, "Wives, submit to your husbands as to the Lord. For the husband is the head of the wife as Christ is the head of the church, his body, of which he is the Savior. Now as the church submits to Christ, so also wives should submit to their husbands in everything." Ephesians 5:28 says for the men, "In the same way, husbands ought to love their wives as their own bodies. He who loves his wife loves himself." It also states in Colossians 3:19 for men, "Husbands, love your wives and do not be harsh with them."

Wives, if you read the Bible, you also should know your part of the marriage. Respect your husband. He is the head of the house, as Christ is the head of the church. Support his decisions. Even if you believe he is in the wrong, pray that the Lord will convict him. Sometimes the job of a spouse is hard, but follow the master plan as best as you can, and God will take care of the rest.

I do not know firsthand yet, but in God's time, he will bless me with a wife, and then I will be put to the test on what I have written and preached. I can't wait! It sounds like a great adventure—as long as I put my relationship with Jesus first and love my wife for what and who she is, not what I think she should be in some unrealistic mental image of a perfect wife.

FOOL'S WISDOM

When I was lost,
I played at no cost.
I lived like a fool,
Thinking I was cool.
I thought I was invincible,
Not knowing God's principles.
I loved women,
But the wrong one was always a lemon.
Learn from the wise.
Let their words not be despised.
At all times pray,
For God's day will not delay.

If you have known the Lord as your Savior since a young age, you might not know where I'm coming from on the following issues. When I was a boy, we went to church every now and then, and in eighth grade, my twin brother and I went through catechism at the Lutheran church we attended. We learned what the Bible said and memorized many verses, but the Word of God was not alive. We were forced to go, so we basically rebelled against it. We didn't want to be there. Even so, I'm happy my parents went ahead with it.

Nevertheless, even after all the human rituals, I was still lost. I still didn't know Jesus on a personal level or really understand salvation. That pastor didn't ask us once if we knew Jesus as our Lord and Savior. My parents divorced about a year later. My brother and I really rebelled. We partied, had sex, tried some drugs, and did just what pleased us. The drugs landed me in the hospital twice. I thank God for the hospital trips because I never touched drugs again in my life. Alcohol and drugs seemed to numb the pain that we were going through at the time.

For two years, I rebelled against my parents, disrespecting them, cursing them, and doing anything to get their goat. They hurt us, so all I wanted to do at that time was to hurt them. But two wrongs don't make a right. I suffered from cranial anal inversion in my younger days, but I took my head out, starting in my senior year of high school. Scripture states in Colossians 3:20, "Children, obey your parents in everything, for this pleases the Lord." Well, I know I did not please the Lord during that time in my life, for I knew it was wrong.

I totally quit drinking and doing drugs. I am a diabetic, and doing these things was not helping my health. When I was drunk, it felt like I was in an insulin reaction. I didn't like it. I still went to parties, but it was to drive people home. It took a while for me to change my attitude toward my parent's decision. Only time can heal a heart that has been hurt.

Ever since I was young, I knew there was something different about me. The Lord had his hands on my life before I even wanted him to, praise God! We all make mistakes, and at times, it seems like we make a heck of a lot more than others do, but God forgives all our sins. Psalm 130:4 backs this up, "But with you there is forgiveness; therefore you are feared."

We also need to remember that we all go through things for reasons. I can witness to people who drink, do drugs, and have experienced divorce. I don't understand all that has happened in my life, and I wish so much that I could take back words and actions, but I can't. I have received forgiveness, and God will use what has happened in my life and yours to touch others with the same kind of problems that we have experienced in our past.

RESTORATION

Restore my soul.
Let my heart not be as coal.
Don't let the rain
Put out my flame.
Encourage me.
Set me free.
Show me your will,
For your will brings me thrills.

Sometimes it seems like all the doors in the world close in on you, no matter what you do, nothing opens up. You have done all you can do to give God a way to work in your life. All Christians, at one point or another, have felt this way. We also feel sometimes like God has taken his presence away from us. He does do this for his own reasons, and most of the time, it is a test to see if we will hold strong to our faith. Yes, God does test us. During your trials, do you believe you pass? Hebrews 11:17 says, "By faith Abraham, when God tested him, offered Isaac as a sacrifice. He who had received the promises was about to sacrifice his one and only son, even though God had said to him, "It is through Isaac that your offspring will be reckoned." So Abraham knowing he already had a promise from God chose to do what God told him to do. Abraham knew God could raise Isaac from the dead, and he would have killed his son by pure-hearted faith. So we all get tested and this is just one scripture that talks of testing one of God's servants.

When these doors keep closing, all we can do is ask God to restore our strength and peace and not to let our hearts grow cold or callused. When the hard times come, and they will, is when God will be with you more than ever.

Some days it seems as if he has left you all alone, but this is a lie from the devil. God is working overtime to help us fulfill our destiny for him, but it will take time. When we pray to be refined by God's fire, it will happen. It is not a joyful time, but a needed time. This is his time to build us up and to make sure our foundations are strong. So try not to worry when those doors close. Isaiah 48:10 says, "See, I have refined you, though not as silver; I have tested you in the furnace of affliction."

There is a reason and purpose behind everything, so let your heart not grow cold. Do not let the devil's lies fool you. It could take years or just merely days for God to answer your prayers, but it is up to us on how we react to the circumstances. When it feels like a thunderstorm in your life, do not let the rain put out your fire.

He does not give or let anything happen to us that we cannot handle. He will give us the strength we need to get through whatever is happening in our life. When we are doing his will, there is no greater peace or thrill. So hang in there and stay strong, and in his time, things will be done.

LINE RIDER

As a cowboy rides the fence line,
He ponders everything to pass the time.
He thinks about God's words in the Bible
And Jesus' next arrival.
The Lord brings his cowboys inspiration
And restoration.
Through grace, there's no cancellation.
The lasting gift is salvation.
Whether on the fence line or bringing in a herd,
A cowboy's praise to God will always be heard.

I love the cowboy way of life and working a ranch. It seems like every cowboy I talk to has so much wisdom. It doesn't matter the topic; cowboys seem to know the right answers to everything. When riding a fence line or bringing in cows, there is a lot of time to pass. So cowboys think about almost everything out there. When I first started to heed God's conviction and sought him more, he brought me around country people and the rodeo circuit. It seems most country people I meet know Jesus as their Lord and Savior.

Country folk tend to bless and help one another out, even when it is competition. If competition cannot pay entry fees for a rodeo, other cowboys or cowgirls would help them out. It seemed like it always came back around to benefit both parties in the end. I fell in love with the atmosphere of how country people worked. They are the hardest working people I've ever met. Country folk work together to get jobs done. Most ranchers team up in the summer months to round up calves and brand. They help one another out and most times do not expect payment. Satisfaction comes from doing a good job for one another and helping out. Repayment most often is receiving help on their branding.

Ranchers receiving help generally have a barbecue and shindig to thank all those who helped get the job done. The environment is so peaceful and enjoyable. I believe that whether you're a cowboy, country person, or city slicker, if you treat one another like this, then the Father will bless you, and your prayers and praise will always be heard. I see country folk putting Mark 12:31 into action more than any other group I see, and it says, "The second is this: 'Love your neighbor as yourself.'" They truly do. It is awesome to see.

ULTIMATE SCORE

Salvation I've scored,
Couldn't have done it without the Lord.
In his hands, my fate rests.
Praise God for the souls in which he invests.
If you do not know him,
You're walking a thin limb.
Let me introduce you.
Salvation doesn't come by sitting in a pew.
It's a one-on-one relationship,
Claiming Jesus as your Lord from your lips.
From your hands, don't let this grace slip away,
For the debt in full has been paid.

John 14:6 says, "Jesus answered, I am the way and the truth and the life. No one comes to the Father except through me." Have you ever thought where this world would be without Jesus and what he did for us on the cross? That's something unthinkable and unbearable. We need to remember that without our salvation, we are nothing! We don't deserve what God did for us, but it was a free gift. Through great love, he offered salvation to us if we want to accept it.

Free will is a gift. This gift could save us or condemn us. God doesn't push his way into our lives. That gift of free will in our conscious would be offended. Praise God, for he cares and he invests in our souls. If you do not believe this, look at what he *let* happen to his only Son on the cross. That was not done for Jesus, but for you and for me!

I believe God convicts every single human on earth and gives us more than enough chances to accept salvation. I know he has followed me around all my life and was always a gentleman. He always sent one of his servants to witness to me one way or another. He never condemned me or said, "That boy has messed up too much, and I will not give him any more chances." Praise God, he never gives up on us. His love is so deep, even when we do not deserve his love!

Some people know about the Lord but think they will have time for him later in their lives. Right now, they are having too much fun pleasing their flesh. An unexpected car accident or a heart attack could take away that *later* syndrome to get right with God. That later will turn into now, and that now turns into too late. Every day that passes, friends and family who don't know Jesus as their Lord and Savior are walking on a thin limb and a thin line.

Whether people want to believe it or not, salvation doesn't come from just sitting in a pew every Sunday, but it comes from understanding what Jesus did for all of us. Truly believing he died on the cross for our sins and saying with their lips, "Jesus is Lord" and believing in their hearts he was raised from the dead. Romans 10:9 states exactly this: "That if you confess with your mouth, 'Jesus is Lord,' and believe in your heart that God raised him from the dead, you will be saved." You *will* be saved if you believe!

When we die, it is too late to repent or ask the Lord into our hearts. On that day, your book in heaven will be closed and stored away until judgment day. So that means we are authors of our own books. Right now, you are writing a chapter.

That day will bring much darkness, pain, and despair. Don't you be on that side, and do your best to witness to everyone you love so they won't either. Jesus paid the debt if you want it now, but wanting it after you die the physical death is too late.

PULLING THROUGH

God, I've done all I can do,
So now I need you to pull through.
I'm at the end of myself.
I'm afraid the stress is affecting my health.
Right now, all I have is hope.
It's hard not to pace around and mope.
Please refresh my spirit,
For your blessings, I know I'm near it.
Give me insight and understanding,
For heaven is my ultimate landing.

Some days are better than others. It seems hope one day can be better than the next. It feels like a rollercoaster ride. Simply do the best that you can do and release the results up to God. This is very hard to do. I learned more about this process while writing this book. The fact of the matter is most of these poems came to me from the Lord within a month. I had no plan of writing this book. It just happened. I was praying for some other things to go through. God works in mysterious ways.

When we come to the end of ourselves, God is able to do the work he wants to do. After we have done what we can do in the physical, it is up to God to make the doors open in the spiritual, which will lead to the manifestation in the physical. We can't open doors ourselves, and if we try, we tend to get burned out from trying. We oftentimes get upset with God because he is not doing things in *our* time. Trying to open doors ourselves usually only leads to being stressed out, depressed, anxious, and very impatient. This affects our relationship with God and loved ones.

Put your hope in God. He knows our heart and will deliver when the time is right. He will refresh you and give you the strength you need. Remember, what seems impossible to us is not impossible for God. Matthew 19:26 says, "With man this is impossible, but with God all things are possible." It doesn't say some things are possible, but *all* things are possible with God.

He put those visions, hopes, and goals into your heart and mind, so it is up to him to see them come to pass. Remember, time here on earth is very short compared to eternity, and we can take nothing with us when we die, with the great exception of our salvation. It is nothing physical we take from this world to heaven, but the spiritual! That is all that is going to heaven, which is the greatest of all, our spirits. Heaven is the landing place, and that is where we need to put our focus.

CONSISTENT

My prayer is the same.
Help me not do things in vain.
Keep me inside from the rain.
Give me peace during the pain.
Help me walk when lame.
I don't ask for fame.
Let me not grow tired of the games.
May your truth remain.
In the Lamb's book, write your names,
In the end, I thank you for remaining the same.

God has callings on our lives, and he put desires and hopes into our hearts. When doing God's will, it will take time. Things in my own experience never happened on my time. That zeal for God and to do his will sometimes feels like it is going to kill me if things don't happen soon. Often, the devil will come in and whisper in your ear, "It will never happen. The dream is too big" and will try to plant the seed of saying, "You're doing things in vain." Sometimes the devil will even use ones closest to you to discourage you. You need to have great discernment on this issue. Romans 8:28 talks about each and every one of us being called. It says, "And we know that in all things God works for the good of those who love him, who have been called according to his purpose."

If what someone is saying agrees with your spirit, then I believe it is God. If it does not agree with your spirit, then take what he or she said to you to the cross and cancel those words out. Or put what he or she said on a shelf and pray about it. The Lord will speak to your heart if it was indeed him speaking through him or her.

Life brings thunderstorms everyday. Don't you wish that when you woke up in the morning, you had a life forecast? I do! It might go something like this, "Today will be partly cloudy. Your mother will call and gossip about what your dad did last month. Then you can look forward to your car breaking down today around 3:00 p.m., and it will only cost you two hundred dollars to fix. But don't worry; your wife will greet you at the door with good news: she is pregnant with triplets, on top of the four kids you already have. Things look like they will clear in the next day or two."

Wouldn't it be great to get a life today report? Hopefully it would sound a little better than that. But that doesn't happen, unfortunately. No matter how bad the thunderstorms seem to get, Jesus remains the same. Hebrews 13:8 says, "Jesus Christ is the same yesterday and today and forever." Even though we don't get a life forecast for the week, stay strong and praise his name. When you heed God's way, your life *is* forecasted. Not heeding his way, you're looking at a lot of scattered thunderstorms in life and eternity. I just hope those storms that blow in your way will lead you to the Father's way. After all, it is up to you how you react to the storms!

FIRST PLACE

Salvation is the prize.
Asking and obedience is the price.
The cost is your pride,
But the destination is precise.
God's grace will pass your pace.
Your will we pursue.
Give us strength during persecution.
By your grace and power,
Let my life be a prayer.
And guide my performance.

All it takes to be saved and assure our space in heaven is for us to ask Jesus to come into our lives and be our Lord and Savior. It is so simple! But many people and the devil complicate things so much. That is one of many master plans of the devil—making everything so complicated. People, things do not get much simpler than asking Jesus to be your savior. Romans 10:9 states, "That if you confess with your mouth, 'Jesus is Lord,' And believe in your heart that God raised him from the dead, you will be saved." It's as simple as that.

Another downfall is the spirit of pride. This is a killer. Proverbs 16:18 says, "Pride goes before destruction, a haughty spirit before a fall." Most people do not want to believe there is a hell. Many believe God wouldn't send them there; then they go out and commit adultery, have orgies, get drunk, curse the one who created them, and so much more. These people also believe they are fine with God, even if his Word says that he hates these things. Don't get me wrong. *No one* is perfect but Jesus himself.

God sends each and every soul several warnings. I believe this with all my heart. He doesn't want to lose one. But the next time he comes will be for judgment.

The evil one is out to deceive. Most have a picture in their mind of what the devil looks like and how he works. But they are deceived already. He is the one telling you, "Hey, she is looking gooood. Let's ask her out and see what could happen later" while your wife and kids are waiting for you at home. He comes in as a liar and deceiver.

There are a few names for him: the devil, Satan, the evil one, demon, or whatever people want to call him.

He comes in many forms. He can speak through your family and friends, girlfriends, boyfriends, husbands, and wives. Satan will show up anywhere that he can discourage you. But do not be mistaken; he is something to be respected. I don't mean to respect him in a good way, but respect him in the way that his schemes are real and deadly. Stay alert and continue to pray for protection over you and your family not to be deceived in any way. 1 Peter 5:8 says, "Be self controlled and alert. Your enemy the devil prowls around like a roaring lion looking for someone to devour."

ENTERTAINMENT?

Entertainment has gone to divorce court.
People have turned ratings into a sport.
Sex on TV is an everyday "thang."
People seem to get a big bang.
They think life is a pro-bono case,
All they can think of is lace.
Shows are out where you can get a wife.
These people really need to get a life.
Be careful of what you fix your eyes on,
Or your life, before you know it, will be gone.
Repent.
Do not relent.
Before we know it, Jesus will be here,
The one we all need to fear.

While flipping through the channels on the TV, I became sick. Our entertainment has gone against the Ten Commandments in every way possible. We as Christians sit and watch these programs and say, "I can't believe they have this on TV." We might not believe it's on TV, but we continue to watch it. Commercials are selling sex, not the product. They have half-naked people promoting what they are trying to sell. The product doesn't stick in a young man's mind, but the image of that half-naked lady does. A lot of people are living by their hormones today.

Little children are watching this stuff. Even the kids' channels will have a lot of these commercials on them. Producers have even made divorce a spectacle on TV as well. This is ridiculous, but people still watch it.

One person that quits watching this trash will have an impact on ratings. How many Christians live in the USA? If we all quit watching these programs, they would have to cancel the shows because of the low ratings. The TV influences people more than ever. Most families consider watching TV family time. This is where the TV is raising your child. Then parents wonder why kids do the things they do and say.

Take the graphic video games and the violence these games promote. Parents let their children play these games and watch these programs so they don't have to deal with them. These, in my opinion, are not games, but teach kids to do violent acts to one another. Whatever happened to Duck, Duck, Goose? Or Hide and Seek? Whatever happened to moms and dads helping their children with homework or spending time teaching their children not to do drugs or telling their kids to wait until marriage for sex? Most parents don't even give the birds and the bees talk anymore, but depend on the public schools to teach them about sex. In my opinion, this is the parents' job.

Parents wonder why their kids do the things they do. One comment I hear is, "What side of the family do you get that from?" Depending on public schools to teach your kids everything they need to know is also wrong. Their job is to teach them how to read and do math. It is up to you as parents to teach the morals. But no one wants to blame themselves for raising their kids; many parents will blame the school system. My aunt is a teacher. Hearing her stories of what parents expect out of teachers makes me sick.

People are now able to get on TV and find their long-lost wife. I'm not too sure about this. I know it is hard to meet dating potentials, but for entertainment purposes, it is going a little extreme. I hope things work out for the ones doing the shows, but making a decision for a lifelong partner in a few weeks is a bit sudden.

I believe everyone who reads this book can agree about how a lot of people are raising their kids. Not everyone raises kids this way, and there are many that do the job right. But the majority depends on others to raise their kids when it is their own responsibility.

Romans 3:18 says, "There is no fear of God before their eyes." Who has the fear of God in them? I hope you do. Because I don't think many do in these days or we would not be seeing what we are seeing in this world right now. Revelation 14:7 says, "He said in a loud voice, 'Fear God and give him glory, because the hour of his judgment has come. Worship him who made the heavens, the earth, the sea and the springs of water.'" Those of us who do not fear God will have a rude awakening someday; I just hope it will not be past the point of no return. If the ones who put this "entertainment" on TV truly feared God, I don't believe we would be seeing what we see. For your health and welfare ... fear God!

MAZE OF LIFE

As I go through this maze called life,
I pray I live not in strife.
I'll make many mistakes,
But I wouldn't want a retake.
Lord, I ask that you develop me,
Into the man you want me to be.
Life seems to be a dream,
Sometimes a little too extreme.
I ask for your guidance.
I'll try to remain silent.
Wisdom, knowledge, and discernment is what I pray,
For these are the end days.
Point me to your ways,
So I will not stray,
Father, please give me favor,
So maybe I can get out on good behavior.
Give me a break,
For my heart is at stake.

A maze explains life pretty well, I think. You have ups and downs and every time you round a corner, another door is in the way. During these times, I pray that I do not grow weary of the maze, but stay strong and continue the course. We all will make more than our fair share of mistakes, but I sure wouldn't want to do it all over again, unless I could with all my lessons learned and wisdom I have now. But that will not happen. Haven't you at least said this once in your life?

When I prayed and asked the Lord to develop me into the man he wants me to be, never would I have thought he would do this so fast! May I also add, he did not do it the way I would have liked him to. Praise God that he does things his way and not ours. It sometimes feels like life is just a dream. I wish I could just float through whatever happened.

This dream and maze we call life can have a bad ending or a great one. We have control over this dream, and it is up to us how our dream will end. Sometimes the dream is way too extreme and seems like the world is ending right now. This is when we need to plug into God's strength. During this dream and maze, we need to continue to ask for guidance and give God room to work. We need to sit down and remain silent. The pain will not last as long. 1 Peter 5:10 says, "And the God of all grace, who called you to his eternal glory in Christ, after you have suffered a little while, will himself restore you and make you strong, firm and steadfast." This is a promise from God—not just empty words! But being in the physical body and mind, we tend to give God our problems, then two hours later, we take it back because he hasn't worked everything out for us in that short period of time.

During these end times, we really need to pray for great discernment. For many are out to deceive and are doing well at it. The one they serve is the master of lies and deceit. We know unfortunately these kinds of people will be blotted out of the Lamb's Book of Life, so earnestly pray that God will keep you safe and on his path to win souls. He will guide us, lead us, and show us, but we need to heed his correction and not stray from his ways that are in the Bible. It is simple; there is a heaven and a hell, and we will be going to one or the other. It is not complex.

If our works saved us, why did Jesus die on the cross?

Read the Holy Bible; it is God's Word, and it will give you all the answers you need.

There are many cults and false beliefs. I pray for the ones involved with false religions or cults, so the truth will prevail in their lives. Go by the Holy Bible, all of it, not parts and pieces. There are so many lies and so little time. The truth will prevail! 1 Timothy 1:3 says,

> As I urged you when I went into Macedonia, stay there in Ephesus so that you may command certain men not to teach false doctrines any longer nor to devote themselves to myths and endless genealogies. These promote controversies rather than God's work—which is by faith. The goal of this command is love, which comes from a pure heart and a good conscience and a sincere faith. Some have wandered away from these and turned to

> meaningless talk. They want to be teachers of the law, but they do not know what they are talking about or what they so confidently affirm.

Beware folks. 1 Peter 5:8 says, "Be self-controlled and alert. Your enemy the devil prowls around like a roaring lion looking for someone to devour."

CROSS FOR THE LOST

Jesus died on the cross.
Still, so many lost.
To what extent is their cost?
Faith is all it takes,
For their souls are at stake.
So many are filled with hate.
Help me keep the pace
With the message of grace.
Let it not be taken in haste.
Lord, I keep our date.
I promise not to be late.
In your hands is my fate.

I have to come to grips with the fact that souls will be condemned. My mission at the beginning of my Christian life was to save everyone. It still is, but I've also realized I can't make people change their ways or make them accept the Lord as their Savior. I can only do what I feel led to do by the Holy Spirit. Then it is God's part to finish and see the seeds flourish.

It hurts to see people going the wrong way. If you tell them, then you are being judgmental and religious, or you're a hypocrite when you mess up. I've heard it said, "I would rather offend you into heaven than comfort you into hell." Believe me, if you witness to people, then you have probably experienced offending someone.

Like I've said before, God gives each and every soul more than enough chances to know the grace he offers. But many have been deceived, whether in the form of another religion or cult or just some spiritual journey some people seem to be on, getting tuned into their spirit. They need to seek the *tuner* instead of the *tuning.* Either way, they will find out the truth and it might not be what they expected or hoped for. Some have also heard the gospel, but did not receive it, or did receive it, but just have not received it with faith. Hebrews 4:2–3 says,

> For we also have had the gospel preached to us, just as they did; but the message they heard was of no value to them, because those who heard did not combine it with faith. Now we who believed enter that rest, just as God has said, "So I declared on oath in my anger, 'They shall never enter my rest.'"

So it is important that we combine what we hear about the true gospel, with faith, or there is no value.

How can people think there is something out there better than the Father and heaven? Satan is a master at disguise and deceiving even the faithful. Mathew 7:15 says, "Watch out for false prophets. They come to you in sheep's clothing, but inwardly they are ferocious wolves." You do the best you can to witness to the lost and keep your date that you have with Jesus. In the end, I know and believe in two destinations: heaven and hell. Which would you prefer? On this vacation, we won't need to pack any bags but one: the bag of salvation. Without that bag, life will be hell. All the sunblock in the world won't help you from getting burned if you do not accept Jesus as your Lord and Savior.

LIFE'S TIDES

As I watch the incoming tides,
I realize life comes in strides.
It comes and goes.
Beginning and end is our souls.
I tend to see people in unknown holes.
Lord, please help them out,
And rid them of their doubt.
Lord, I want to bless.
Help me rebuke the evil pest.
I want to help house, clothe, and feed,
For there is a need.
Deliver your help with speed
And help me plant eternal seeds.

Tides of the ocean come in and out every day, seven days a week. It has a certain time when it comes and goes. In a way, life is like this. The tide will come in and seem to drown you, but just at the last second, it's time for the tide to head back out. I've only been to the ocean a handful of times, but it was amazing how fast tides showed up and how fast they left. Problems in life also have a way of showing up out of nowhere. But at the same time, when we praise the Father and glorify his name, they tend to leave in a hurry also. There will be ups and downs in life, but in the very end, everything will be worth it. Remember, at the end, everything will come together for the purpose of God.

We always want to understand things, but in my experience, we will never understand things during the trial; we must wait until after the trial. In the very beginning of our lives, we have our souls; during our lives, we have our souls. At the very end, we still have our souls. What good is your soul if it is going to hell? It would have been better not to have even been born.

But we don't have the control of being born, do we? We do have the power and control over where our soul is going, however. Our lives and the one and only soul we have for eternity will be spent in either heaven or hell, which is the second biggest gift God gave us. The first is Jesus dying on the cross; his blood did away with the old covenant and produced a new one. Hebrews 9:18–22 says, "This is why even the first covenant was not put into effect without blood. When Moses had proclaimed every commandment of the law to all the people, he took the blood of calves, together with water, scarlet wool and branches of hyssop, and sprinkled the scroll and all the people. He said, "This is the blood of the covenant, which God has commanded you to keep." In the same way, he sprinkled with the blood both the tabernacle and everything used in its ceremonies. In fact, the law requires that nearly everything be cleansed with blood, and without the shedding of blood there is no forgiveness." So without blood in the first covenant or the second covenant, there is no forgiveness. Jesus was the ultimate sacrifice and the only sacrifice we get. So where we go for eternity is in your power. If you don't witness to your loved ones, who will?

Seeing people struggling really grabs my heart. Everyone thinks that the hole he or she is in is deeper than everyone else's. We seem to think our problems are bigger and badder than the other person's are. Well, they are in a way—in the way that those problems are what we are going through at that time and we don't know how to get through them.

There is *no unknown* problem that someone else hasn't already fought through before you. Listen to people and give them comfort during their hard times. That is where they get comfort—someone simply listening to them. When we feel all alone in the world, fighting a battle by ourselves will wear us out and make us feel hopeless. Bless people during their trials, and you will be blessed and comforted during yours.

If you see a homeless person, bless him in any way that the Father speaks to your heart. Buy him a bag of groceries or a blanket or even better, introduce him to Jesus. God will speak to your heart about what he needs. Just seek his will and heed the conviction you get. Whatever you do, bless one another and love one another. Quit arguing about things that you will not remember a month from now. Mark 12:33 says, "To love him with all your heart, with all your understanding and with all your strength, and to love your neighbor as yourself is more important than all burnt offerings and sacrifices." So quit bickering and start loving and reaching out anyway you can. You never know, you one day may need that love or helping hand.

HIS PATH

Lord Most High,
I draw nigh.
In your peace, I confide.
Help me keep pace at your stride.
Your Holy Spirit fire
Is my heart's desire.
Persecution, help me endure.
Keep me away from the impure.
Guide my words when I preach.
The Holy Spirit, I pray, to teach.

When we draw close to God, he draws close to us. When we get to that intimate closeness, there is a peace that can overcome anything that is happening in our lives. That peace is what I strive for everyday. The mind is the enemy's playground. He puts so much trash into our minds that sometimes it's hard to keep up with rebuking him. Rest assured, the battle has already been won. Satan's doom will come to a fiery eternity soon enough. Hang in there, and do not entertain evil and lustful thoughts.

Keeping up with God's stride is very important. The devil will entertain your mind with evil thoughts and try to get you off God's path. Do not put those thoughts into actions. Entertaining thoughts is sinful enough, and acting on those thoughts is just plain sin. Confine your mind to Jesus and *nothing* will be impossible for you, because nothing is impossible with God. Luke 1:37 says exactly that, "For nothing is impossible with God." So even if things do seem tough, or impossible ... remember, it's not with God.

Have you ever heard that you become like whom you hang around? Well, it is true. The part that I wrote about "Keep me away from the impure" means exactly that. I don't want to hang around people that gossip or stab one another in the back. You can bet your house that if they do that to others, you can count on the same sort of treatment once you walk away. With friends like that, who needs enemies?

I'm not perfect or trying to act like it, but I do expect a lot out of myself. We all sin and not one of us can throw the first stone. Romans 3:23 says, "for all have sinned and fall short of the glory of God, and are justified freely by his grace through the redemption that came by Christ Jesus." It's all grace and mercy. When I do witness, I want the Holy Spirit to speak through me. The life I choose to live will also witness, so I try not to ruin anything God is trying to do through me. We just need to do the best we can do. God knows we will make mistakes.

COWBOY LIFE

Life as a cowboy
Means days without pay,
Miles on the highway,
Eating fast food,
Kids calling you "dude,"
Fixing flat tires,
Or stringing up barbed wire,
Getting on bulls,
That want to crush your skull,
Sweating in the sun
While friends are out having fun.
The only pay
Comes from bringing in the hay.
This cowboy wouldn't want it any other way.

This poem was just for fun. It takes two aspects of most cowboys' lives: rodeo and working on a ranch. On the rodeo part of it, if you don't win a rodeo or day money, you may get hungry, unless you have some good partners to give you a loan, which was usually the case for me. For a rookie in the pros, survival can be very tough. If you don't have a sponsor, traveling the road and equipment costs can run you back home, unless you have the heart for it. I tried pro for two years. It was a lot of fun, but I didn't have the heart or finances to carry on. One thing that was tiring was eating fast food. You get to missing a good, home-cooked meal.

I'm just talking about how I experienced the road. I really didn't have it as bad as others did because I only went to a few pro shows. I still worked for a living during the week and went to weekend shows and some during the week if they were close. But let me tell you, if you like a good rush, get on a bull that wants to poke you with his clown pokers or a bareback horse that wants to jerk your arm out of your socket. That is *fun!* Sick, I know, but it is. The rush for me was the not knowing, not knowing if you will make the whistle or literally lose your life. You are on an animal that has its own mind. When I'm old and gray, at least I can say I've tried everything I wanted to.

The other side of life for a cowboy is working a ranch. It is by far some of the hardest work out there. When you are at a job, at least you get a weekly paycheck. For the majority of ranchers, the job needs to be complete before a profit comes in. It all depends on if they raise cattle, train horses, or run a farm and plant crops. It is a tough way to make a living.

If you like security, this might not be your line of work. These people do need our prayers. The majority of the time, the man works the farm or ranch and the wife works a normal job to keep the food on the table and clothes on the back. Plus, she still does chores on the farm. This is a family effort. Everyone in the family has a duty. Not one duty is less than the other. If one is not done, then it could ruin the whole program and their livelihood. These people are the hardest working and most loving people I've met. May God bless them all and give them peace and strength to carry on!

HE KNOWS

How can God know?
Every river that flows,
Every hair on my head,
Every book that's been read,
Every grass in the meadows,
Every child in the ghettos,
Every battle fought,
Every deal bought,
Every creature,
Every feature,
How can God know?
He created it!

Have these questions ever come to your mind? They have for me, obviously. Sometimes it's good to sit down and really think about what we are striving for. The will of God? Our own success? Love? Humility? How can we bless? What motivates you when you get out of bed?

We can't even comprehend what God knows. He created everything. Every rock, grain of sand, tree, creature, and even the number of hairs on them. Wow! Have you ever really thought about it? It blows my mind! So if he knows all of this information, don't you think he knows what we are going through? Yes, he does know what we are going through becasue he knows all!

We can't hide from him. Isaiah 29:15 says, "Woe to those who go to great depths to hide their plans from the Lord, who do their work in darkness and think, "Who sees us? Who will know?" You turn things upside down, as if the potter were thought to be like the clay! Shall what is formed say to him who formed it, "He did not make me?" Can the pot say of the potter, "He knows nothing?" We can run, but what is the use? Think about it. He knows every snowflake that falls, every drop of rain. I could go on, but stop a minute and think about these things. Did you do it? Take a minute. Go ahead. This book isn't going anywhere. Come on; do it!

I wonder how many people actually stopped when I first asked. I believe that would be an interesting fact to know. That is why God has to send so many prophets and warnings because it takes us several times to hear or until something bad happens to catch our attention. Try having God's agenda for a day. Everything under the sun, God knows all about it. He knows all our secrets, all our hearts' desires, and all our true intentions. So let all you do be true and pure in God's sight!

SHACKLES OF SIN

On our feet are shackles of sin.
With them, blessings we cannot win.
They limit our steps
And pull us down to the depths.
This is Satan's plan.
Resist, and it cannot stand.
Break free.
Open your eyes and see.
Your breakthrough has been won.
When Jesus raised, it was done.
In faith, stand firm.
You will then see Satan squirm.
Then the shackles will be broken,
But from you, the words need to be spoken.

We all, at one point or another, have carried shackles of sin around. If you can picture yourself in shackles in the physical, then you have a good idea how it is in the spiritual. When we carry shackles of unforgiveness, adultery, idolatry, or any other sin, we tend to cut off the life-giving force from our Father.

The devil will use condemnation over you when you carry these or any shackles of sin. The enemy will make you feel like it is impossible to break through. Remember that Satan is here to steal, kill, and destroy. He is not a gentleman and does not care how he can trouble you. When we leave a small door open, he will see to it that it ends up being a garage door.

Not one of us will be sinless, except Jesus himself. God knows this; he knows what you will do before you do it. Sad, huh? But he will turn everything around for his purpose. Shackles of sin are just what the enemy needs to suck us down into depression, anxiety, stress, or, again, anything he can do to get us away from the purpose of God. I'm not saying that if you suffer from some of the above that it is a satanic attack because of your sin; there are medical conditions that do cause these, but a lot of times these are tools of his, and he can pull us down into the depths with one simple mistake we make.

The good news is that we have power over what the devil throws our way. Luke 10:19–20 says, "I have given you authority to trample on snakes and scorpions and to overcome all the power of the enemy; nothing will harm you. However, do not rejoice that the spirits submit to you, but rejoice that your names are written in heaven." We gained that power the day Jesus rose from the grave and conquered all the devil's evil schemes. Do not let Satan tell you how hard it is to resist him. It is so simple, but we always tend to make things more complex than they really are. All we have to do is draw near to God. Rebuke Satan and bind him away in the name of Jesus and by the blood of Jesus. When you command Satan and his demons away from you, they *have* to leave. No excuses. They will try to come back, but keep rebuking and binding. Mathew 12:43–45 says this, "When an evil spirit comes out of a man, it goes through arid places seeking rest and does not find it. Then it says, "I will return to the house I left.' When it arrives, it finds the house unoccupied, swept clean and put in order. Then it goes and takes with it seven other spirits more wicked than itself, and they go in and live there." Do it as much as it takes. When we stand firm in our faith, the enemy squirms and can't stand it. Because when we are firm, Satan can't shake us. So make up your mind that the enemy cannot touch your faith. Faith can only waiver if we let it. *Praise God* in your tough times! That frustrates the enemy more than *anything!*

END DAYS

We have arrived at the end days.
God's purpose will not delay.
Ask Jesus to be your Lord and Savior.
Pray your faith will not waiver.
Invest in future rewards.
Eternal life these will go towards.

If you have been watching the news lately, then you can see Bible prophecy passing us by at a rapid pace. In my heart, I believe without a doubt that we are in the end days. Some do not agree, but I'm looking at the signs of the times, and they tell me we are close. Close could be a hundred years from now or a thousand. Or maybe tomorrow; I don't know. All I do know is that we are closer than we were yesterday. *Only* the Father knows. But I think we are closer than many want to believe.

Some say, "I am not ready to go yet. I still have things to do." Well, we all better get those things done tomorrow because God isn't going to confer with us to see if the timing is good.

Ask Jesus to be your Lord and Savior if you do not know him. You might go to church on Christmas and Easter, folks, but that doesn't mean you're saved, and it doesn't mean you're not. What matters is if you believe that Jesus was God's only Son, he died on the cross for your sins, and three days later he rose from the dead. Life will only be a great gift if you receive Jesus as your Savior! For those who don't know, Jesus is alive and well today, as he was over two thousand years ago.

In these end days, pray that your faith will not waiver because it probably will be tested. Invest in doing good and bless others, for this will store up treasures in heaven for you. Be careful whom and what you listen to, and if the answers you get don't feel right, question them! If you read the Bible, then what you are witnessing on the news about all that is happening in Israel and the Middle East is right on queue. Jesus warns us of the things to come and what to watch for in Matthew 24:6–8: "You will hear of wars and rumors of wars, but see to it that you are not alarmed. Such things must happen, but the end is still to come. Nation will rise against nation, and kingdom against kingdom. There will be famines and earthquakes in various places. All these are the beginning of birth pains."

These are physical warnings that we are able to see. There is also a huge spiritual war that we can't see. That war is for your soul! Times are short and will get tough; salvation is your only insurance policy to make it through whatever comes your way. Jesus is the insurance policy, but he will not rip you off. He is the *only* fire insurance you are able to get and afford. His policy only costs faith! Romans 3:22 says, "This righteousness from God comes through faith in Jesus Christ to all who believe."

THE BLOOD

By the blood of the Lamb,
We are not damned.
Follow God's instruction.
It will keep you from destruction.
We are not saved by deeds,
Nor because God has the need,
But because of his undying love
That descends like a dove.
He created you
His love reigns.
By it, eternal life we gain.

Jesus died on the cross as our ultimate sacrifice. By his blood, the old covenant God had with his people was canceled and the new one took its place. Covenants are binding by blood. The old covenant required sacrifices made by people and priests for the forgiveness of their sin. Sacrifices were animals, and their blood sealed God's old covenant. When Jesus died on the cross and was raised from the dead, it meant people no longer had to make sacrifices here on earth because Jesus was the ultimate sacrifice. We now have God's grace for the forgiveness of sin through his *only* Son! 2 Corinthians 3:14 says, "But their minds were made dull, for to this day the same veil remains when the old covenant is read. It has not been removed, because only in Christ is it taken away." This scripture is talking about his chosen people, Israel. They still do not believe Jesus was the Messiah and that a Messiah is still to come. The veil will not go away until they realize Jesus Christ is their Savior and was their Messiah.

But we have to ask him to forgive us. So by Jesus' blood, we are not condemned, and we are given the free gift of salvation that God gave to us through his love and grace through Jesus. By Jesus you will live eternal life or live in eternal hell. Do not let your heart be hardened from your hard times nor let the enemy come in and discourage you. Follow God's commandments, and you will be blessed and saved from the wrath that will pour out on ones that do not believe in Jesus. For the ones who worship other so-called gods, they will meet the same end as Satan.

These other so-called gods could be money, sex, idolatry, etc. God didn't have to send his only Son, and he didn't have to give salvation to us either. But he loves us. He is our Father, and that is what a Father would do for his children.

What we do in life will be judged. What we do determines our rewards in heaven. What you do will *not* get you eternal life with the Father. Matthew 16:27 states exactly this: "For the Son of Man is going to come in his Father's glory with his angels, and then he will reward each person according to what he has done."

The bottom line is this: just believe that God sent his only begotten Son to die for you. He is real and alive today! Don't you want to meet your Father? We will never be able to understand his love until we get to heaven. Please, get to know God in a personal relationship. Don't practice religion, but seek a personal relationship, like with your husband or wife, but there is no arguing with God because he is *always right!*

HIS PLANS

I strive
To be alive,
Yet to fulfill my vows,
For I don't know how
I promised to help bring Jesus souls.
This path, I do not just want to stroll.
Lord, I want to bless
And live life not in stress.
Tell me, Father, your plan.
Give me your blueprints to get every woman and man,
So everlasting life they will taste,
So life in general was not a waste.

So many of us strive everyday just to stay alive spiritually. Some days are good and some are bad. We have to fight off emotional attacks everyday. Believers in Jesus have security, the security of knowing that he has already won the battle. Also, once everything is said and done, we will be heading to eternal glory to spend the rest of our forever in a place with no pain or suffering.

I have no idea what heaven will be like, but I can guarantee it will be better than a lifetime at a Sandals Resort. Now, that does sound pretty nice, but heaven will blow that illusion away.

When we make vows to God, we usually make promises that are humanly impossible to achieve ourselves. God knows this, and he will help you achieve what you have promised. He knows what is in your heart, and he planted those ideas and visions in there. But he also needs time to mature you to do these things.

I have a hard time if I'm not out witnessing or blessing someone. I do not just want to take a stroll on God's path, but I want to sprint. I feel like a racehorse that is stuck in the starting gate. Praise God for doing this. I'm sure if God didn't hold me back, I would mess up pretty bad. Remember, we are now representatives of God!

I don't know your zeal for God, but for me, I can hardly stand it. I don't just want to observe on a fence! I don't want to be lukewarm; give me hot! Revelation 3:16 says, "So, because you are lukewarm—neither hot nor cold—I am about to spit you out of my mouth." One side or the other folks, we can't be on both. I want the Holy Spirit to sit on my head and whack me across the head when I mess up or become lukewarm. I always want God to deliver what I pray for in rapid speed, but he keeps holding me back, saying, "Take it easy, son. Let me prepare you for what I've already prepared for you."

So I let out a sigh and say, "Okay, God. Forgive me. I'm sorry."

I'm sure happy he doesn't answer my prayers on my time because my time is almost always the wrong time. But he does answer prayers on *his* time! Psalm 120:1 says, "I call on the Lord in my distress, and he answers me." But are you prepared or ready for what you pray for? If God does not think so, you will not get that answer until his time is right.

THE DEALER

In my heart, I want to be used as a healer.
But the Lord is the dealer.
If I play my cards right,
The Lord will fly me like a kite.
Be humble,
Not always ready to rumble.
God will not let me stumble
Even when I have fumbled.
God, direct my path.
Keep me from your wrath.
God, open the sky
And please give me your reply.

John 14:12 says, "I tell you the truth, anyone who has faith in me will do what I have been doing. He will do even greater things than these, because I am going to the Father." I truly take this promise to heart. I want the Lord to be able to use me like he used Peter and many of his faithful and unfaithful disciples. What I mean by unfaithful is that his disciples also struggled with faith. Look at Peter. He denied Jesus three times, even in front of him.

Praise God, for he forgives and will use us greatly for his purposes. Jesus says that people who have *faith* in him will do greater things. But you have to *believe* that God can do what you ask him to do—he can, and much more. My opening of the poem states that I want to be used as a healer. I know he can do this, and I want to be able to have his trust to pray for healings without me getting a big head. He can, and he will. Do not get a big head when great favor from God is flowing through you, but *praise* him and give him the glory. He will do more. The minute we think we did all that God is doing through us is the time we will lose that favor.

When we stay humble, God will fly us like a kite. You will go higher and farther than you ever have. Don't be stubborn and always ready to grumble or argue. It is a waste of time. James 5:9 says, "Don't grumble against each other, brothers, or you will be judged. The judge is standing at the door." God will not use you if you do these things. Can you blame him? If you want to play gossip or politics, he will find someone else that will obey his decrees and not waste his time.

After all, God has all the time in the world. But we are the ones running out. We will stumble and fumble the ball sometimes, but God will be there to make sure we are able to pick that ball back up and run for a touchdown! He does direct our paths, so don't fret, but keep still and always be ready for God to use you. He will need you at a time when you least expect it.

HOLY LAW

God's law
Has no flaw.
At first sight,
You lose all fleshly rights.
It doesn't seem tame,
But God's love remains the same.
So enjoy the ride,
And to God's law abide,
For you will see good days,
And God's blessings will not delay.

God's commandments do not have one flaw. Psalm 12:6 says, "And the words of the Lord are flawless, like silver refined in a furnace of clay, purified seven times." They are simple and very easy to understand. But we humans try to introduce loopholes into God's law. Loopholes are for man's law, not God's. We also have humans deceiving many people with cults and false religions. Where does this come from? Satan!

Some religions don't believe in hell. Well, it's in the Bible, and if you don't believe that God would create a hell, then you better play it safe and ask Jesus into your heart right now so you don't have to find out the hard way. Complicating the understanding of heaven and God's law is another tool used by the evil one. He tries to deceive people into what sounds good to them and not the facts.

At first sight of God's law, you have the privilege of losing all fleshly rights. Your life and body are no longer your own. For you were bought at a price. First Corinthians 6:19–20 says, "You are not your own; you were bought at a price. Therefore honor God with your body." That price was Jesus dying on the cross for your sins and giving you a freedom that will not come from anywhere else.

Does losing what you are used to sound inviting to you? Well, it didn't to me when I first met the Lord. There was a lot of confusion and hardly any understanding, even growing up Lutheran. To me, as a nonbeliever living in sin for so long, asking Jesus into my life was a hard step to take and a hard one to understand. It doesn't seem inviting or tame at first, but that is what the devil wants a nonbeliever to think. At first you think, *What exactly can I do?* The enemy does not want to lose any souls that he has spent so much time on. To repent from sin and accept God's grace and the forgiveness of your sin means Satan just lost you. He will tell people that it is too late for them to repent and they can't stay away from fleshly pleasure, whatever the pleasure may be.

Another lie is, "Oh, you're okay with God. You don't murder or anything like that." If you do not apply God's principles, then you are not okay with God! If you don't ask Jesus to be your personal savior, then you are not okay with God. That is a false hope the enemy is feeding you! God's love remains the same for you whether you're a sinner or a believer. His love does not change; we do. We are being tempted everyday and lured away from the truth with lies.

You do what you need to do to get right with God because tomorrow may be too late. Don't be misled from the truth. Obey God's law and you will see blessings pour out on you. Don't miss out on the biggest and best gift, the gift of salvation.

ONLY ONCE

It won't happen twice.
We only get one sacrifice.
If you pass this one by,
For eternity you will fry.
Respect the cross.
Don't let it be your loss.
Call on his name today.
Do not delay,
For time is running out.
And there is no other route.

Jesus dying on the cross will only happen once. The Bible says that Jesus is God's *only* begotten Son. God does not have a second son to give as a sacrifice. Our sins only need to be justified once through the blood of Jesus. But again, that is a decision that is up to you. Hebrews 7:27 says, "Unlike the other high priests, he does not need to offer sacrifices day after day, first for his own sins, and then for the sins of the people. He sacrificed for their sins once for all when he offered himself."

So if you or anyone you know passes up this opportunity, then eternity will be looking grim. This is no joke! It is the truth, straight up and no beating around the bush. We can beat around that salvation bush all we want, but if we do not tell it how it really is, people's future for eternal life is not looking good.

Praise God, Moses didn't beat around that burning bush! Don't let anyone you know or love pass on this *one and only* sacrifice and salvation God offers now. The next time Jesus comes is not to have mercy, but to judge the living and the dead. Acts 10:42 says, "He commanded us to preach to the people and to testify that he is the one whom God appointed as judge of the living and the dead." For the dead, their fate is sealed. Is your fate sealed? I only hope and pray I'm all right with the Lord and heaven bound.

We need to respect what Jesus did for us on the cross. Once people pass this opportunity up, it will be too late to make the right decision when they're dead. Do not let this chance slip away. We have no other choices on where we spend eternity. Heaven and hell are the only two choices we have.

The map Jesus left behind will lead you to more

treasure than the entire world holds, and it's *free*. Take it! The map is the Bible, and the treasure is salvation!

WORD'S POWER

Words have power.
And Some are sour.
They can bless,
Or take away stress.
Let words not promote weakness.
If your words don't encourage, stay speechless.
So watch what you say,
For harsh words can never be taken away.

Have you ever had to nurse a curse? I know for a fact everyone in this world has had to do this. What I mean by nursing a curse is when someone tells you something like, "You can't do that" or "That's stupid" or "What were you thinking?" or basically any word to plant into your head you can't do something or you're weak.

People put curses on one another every day without even realizing it, and some simply know when they are cursing you but do not care. They come from husbands, wives, boyfriends, girlfriends, friends, brothers, sisters, or anyone. Simple words should not be a curse, but many times people say curses without knowing it because they have done it all their lives.

When someone speaks a curse over you, take it to the cross, and by Jesus' blood, cancel the curse. Let them know their words cursed you, and have them also take those words to the cross. People, your words bless, curse, discourage, or encourage people's lives. Watch what you say. Bless the ones you love. Don't curse them or their ability to do something. What may seem impossible to you is not impossible with God, and he may have anointed that person to do his will that may seem impossible to you.

Many times, I believe God's will does not get done because of the curses loved ones put on us. The majority of the time, they don't mean to, but it will plant a seed in our heads that the dream is too big or we're not smart enough or don't have the experience. The list goes on and on. Do you see and understand what I'm talking about?

There are books out there that explain curses a lot better and in more detail. This is just a taste. Promote encouraging words to one another. This society is so used to negativism that we just seem to have adopted it right into our everyday lives.

Take the news, for instance. When was the last time you heard about the Boy Scout helping the little old lady across the street? Or when September 11th happened, Americans, for a short time, forgot all about their differences and pulled together. Eventually we hear on the news how organizations stole millions of dollars from gifts given to aid the victims' families. People, just because there are a few bad apples doesn't mean they all are. We just tend to hear about the ones that are trying to ruin the crop.

Watch your words, for they have more power than you will ever know. God created the universe with words! What kind of words do you like to hear? Encouraging or discouraging? If a person hears that he is stupid enough times, he starts to believe it's true. The words we speak today will have an impact on someone's life tomorrow. Words are not easily forgotten, if ever.

HIS DEAL

God created the constellation Orion
And all of Africa's lions.
Everything in the heavens and earth,
He has created and given birth.
Don't ever feel
That you have accomplished the deal.
To God and others, respect.
In later days, this could protect.
Always stay humble
And do not grumble,
For the day will come soon
When blood will be the moon. Joel 2:31

God has created every grain of sand and dirt we walk on. He knows every single one of them and every hair on every animal and human. It's pretty hard to comprehend that little bit of information, isn't it? But it's true. He knows every single star hanging in the sky and every one that has fallen. He knows what is truly in peoples' hearts—the good and the bad. We cannot hide from our God, but we always want to believe that we have a little privacy. Impossible! He knows what we do in the dark, the light, and every single corner we round. He gave life to each and every living thing, including plankton! You know, the little things you looked at in science class under a microscope in seventh grade? I could go on, but I believe you know what my message is stating. He knows all! Genesis 1:30 says, "And to all the beasts of the earth and all the birds of the air and the creatures that move on the ground-everything that has the breath of life in it-I give every green plant for food. And it was so."

When the Lord blesses you with spiritual gifts, or finances, or a big heart, he wants you to use those gifts to glorify his name, not yours. 1 Corinthians 12:4–6 says, "There are different kinds of gifts, but the same spirit. There are different kinds of service, but the same Lord. There are different kinds of working, but the same God works all of them in all men." So there are different gifts, but the same spirit, Lord, and God who chooses to distribute them as he sees fit. Those business deals you prayed for that you thought you couldn't make without a miracle? Yep, he was there and made it happen. So whether you're rolling in the dough or laying hands on the sick and the Lord heals them, do not ever think that you got there yourself. I believe that you earned those privileges and gained God's favor and trust with a pure heart, but it was *not* done by your power.

Have you ever heard the saying, "Don't burn any bridges"? Most people have, and it is a brilliant saying. Respect God and his only begotten Son for what they did for us. If you respect him and love him, in your hard times, you will find favor and incredible peace and strength. This can also go well with you from a human point of view. We will never know what lies around the corner for ourselves. If you show favor to the needy, it seems as if it always comes back around and you are blessed. So, don't burn any bridges!

Blessings do not always consist of giving money, they can be emotions or prayers or anything people are lacking at the time. Never expect repayment when you give. Let it be a blessing, and in the long term, it will come back! Do not gossip or grumble behind one's back, for it will never profit you in any way.

In Joel 2:31 it says, "The sun will be turned to darkness and the moon to blood before the coming of the great and dreadful day of the Lord." The day is coming soon, and you do not want to be wasting your time on things that will not glorify the Father and the kingdom of heaven. *So bless one another!*

UNTIL DEATH

When you find a husband or wife,
God intends you to keep them for life.
Marriage is not easy.
Some days will make you queasy.
Things will get rough.
Some days you'll think it's enough.
Recall "for better or worse"
Or until you ride in a hearse?
Divorce is not a shortcut,
But only later digs a deeper rut.
During trials, the Lord will help.
Finish the hand you dealt.
After all, your partner you chose.
God didn't drop to his knee and propose.
Finish what you started.
What God let be joined, never let be parted.

When you are standing at the altar making your vows to God and your mate, the last thing you are thinking about is the hard times you will eventually encounter. I come from a divorced family. The image that I had throughout my childhood of having a perfect family (except a few fights every now and then) was shattered.

I am twenty-nine years old at the time of writing this book, and I'm still not married. I have waited a long time to make sure I get what I want in a partner. You will never find a *perfect* spouse, but make sure the one you pick is the one you will die with. It will take time, and you will go through a few dates before you find the one, but relax. He or she is usually right around the corner.

For those already married, I know some days you want to put on tennis shoes and run out of your marriage, but you made a vow to God and to your spouse. In Numbers 30:2, it says, "When a man makes a vow to the Lord or takes an oath to obligate himself by a pledge, he must not break his word but must do everything he said." It does not say, "He can" or "It's okay to not fulfill your vows." It says, "He must *not* break his word but must do everything he said." Among believers, the divorce rate is as high as nonbelievers and for most of the same reasons: adultery, lust, boredom, careers, finances, no communication or whatever the excuse is! What does God have to say about divorce? Malachi 2:16 says this, "I hate divorce," says the Lord God of Israel, "and I hate a man's covering himself with violence as well as with his garment," says the Lord Almighty."

Go to counseling and do not quit until you both feel

you have been heard and come up with solutions and both are applying them. Things don't happen overnight so quit thinking they should. It didn't happen overnight that landed you in the situation that your currently in now. So give each other some encouragement and forgiveness along the way. Just because you demand something, don't expect perfection overnight on their part if you yourself cannot be perfect. Otherwise no one is perfect but Jesus and give your partner some leniency!

If one wants to try, but the other does not, unfortunately it will not work out. The person putting in the effort will start to resent the other and things get ugly, and you say and do things that are not Christian. But the other person thinks they are trying just as hard as you are, and they more than likely are, but not in the way you think they should, and this is wrong on your part if you think it is always the other person's fault. This is what happened to me in my last relationship. I didn't think she was trying and that I was the only one trying, and I was wrong. She felt the same way. So our try never seemed good enough for each other. This is the enemy, not God.

My mouth would overrun my mind and heart and say things that were out of frustration, anger and hurt. I was then in the wrong. Two wrongs do not make a right. Nor does one right and one wrong make a right. But action on both parties make a right when they come together and find a solution. It may not be exactly what you think it should be, but we need to find some common ground. Love people how you want to be loved. Knock your walls down, and let people in. Don't live in the past where you were hurt before and then put that blame onto innocent people who hope to find a home in your heart. If you don't take those walls down from your heart, you will always have what you currently have ... failure and loneliness.

Quitting is never easy; maybe at the time it seems so, but the problems do not disappear when we quit or run away. You can also see a track record. Were they engaged before? Who ran out in previous relationships? What was the cause of no success? What is the cause of no success this time? More often than not, it will be for basically the same reason of the other failures or something to do with the previous failures. Do you expect too much from your partner? Do you think you can change them?

There are deep rooted issues in us all. For some, it shows in all relationships, and for others, they have forgiven and moved on. This is not a put down! Some of us need professional help to deal with some hurts. The hurt is real. Hurt will stay with you until you want it gone. Or you can pretend the hurt is not real, or the best solution is to face them head on. Face what is currently in your life here and now. Moving on to someone else does, in no way, cure anything. For it will rear its ugly head again in time.

Most people, I think, justify their actions by telling themselves that it is everyone else who has the issues and they were the only ones wronged. But it does take two, and we all need to remember just that. It does take two! But if you see something in a relationship that scares you that has happened in the past, it is how you will react to the issue that will get you either the same results as always or the result you want. Don't let that fear turn into anger and resentment. God has a way to bring things back around to us until we meet the issues head on. Unfortunately the quitter loses out on a lot of life, joy, and who knows what else, in my opinion.

I know these types of people are loved if they would just accept it. They often will just look at your bad side and things you have done wrong and tell themselves that you're a jerk so it will be easier for them to quit or run away. They also will tell this to their family and friends so they feel justified in their run. There is so much more going on in the inside of people who do this, but we can't help unless they want the help and ask for it and make the continuous effort to find solutions. Otherwise, we will be along for the ride until that happens, or they simply choose to move on.

God gave us a roadmap to get through life, but we all still want to go our own way and follow our own desires. This road will only bring more misery. My parents divorced when my brother and I were in tenth grade. Unless you have been through a divorce, words cannot explain what it does to kids. They are victims. Many people believe their problems will vanish when they get divorced or run from a relationship. But from what I have witnessed and experienced, it only causes more grief and hurt. I just witnessed the problems carry on into the next marriage or relationship. If people cannot work out the first marriage and those problems, what makes people think they can succeed in another?

Often they will succeed, but it is because they actually decide to put in the effort that should have been put into the first relationship. But it is just as hard or harder, because they chose to wait so long to confront their issues. But it is when they decide enough is enough and make up their mind that they want success instead of failure. After all, those problems still exist and always will until this happens. You only walk right into a new spouse's problems and his or her past, so that effort, more times than not, will need to be greater.

In my mind, it just doesn't make sense. The hurt will never leave; how can it? We will always be reminded during the holidays or family functions. Who should we go spend the holidays with?

I will never understand why people hurt one another and give up so quickly. Praise God, he didn't give up on us! The only thing I can do now for myself and suggest to others is accept it and forgive your parents or the ones who have hurt us so much. After all, they only have one life to figure things out as we do. We also make mistakes. We tend to look at our parents' mistakes and do the opposite with our own children. But one extreme will lead to a different extreme. So who is really right? Forgive because you have been forgiven!

ONE WAY

Many Christians backslide.
Opinions make a church divide.
Unity, we should all be in one.
Do we all believe in Jesus, the begotten Son?
If you can't back your theory in the Bible,
You can know your opinion is from the rival.
Don't interpret things to match your way,
For the life we run is our only relay.
Pray to God for better insight,
For he will answer with delight.

Many Christians, including myself, seem to backslide every now and then, more now than then. We tend to lose touch with the Holy Spirit and do things our way. When plans don't go the way we had hoped, or they completely fail, we come back to God and ask for his advice and help. I wish I didn't have to do things the hard way, but it seems the only way to learn is to fail at my way, repent, and ask God for his way.

We all will backslide every now and then and make mistakes. But nowhere in the Bible did I read life was going to be easy. In fact, several passages in the Bible tell us we will be tempted and life will, at times, be hard. God warns us so many times throughout our lives and in his Word, but that wonderful gift of free will tends to get many of us into a lot of trouble.

I talk with many Christians, and many Christians have so many different ideas. A new believer can get confused with all the different opinions out there. Using tongues is an example. A new believer can read the full truth about speaking in tongues in the Old Testament and in the New Testament. But many Christians don't believe in speaking in tongues. Some say tongues were only spoken in the early church and God doesn't give that gift anymore.

I'm sorry, but I'm pretty black and white when it comes to conversations like this one. First Corinthians 12:4–6 says, "There are different kinds of gifts, but the same spirit. There are different kinds of service, but the same Lord. There are different kinds of working, but the same God works all of them in all men." So the Bible, God's Word and law, is saying there are many kinds of gifts but the same spirit. The same Lord and the same God distributes each gift to each person as he sees fit.

First Corinthians 14:5 says, "I would like every one of you to speak in tongues, but I would rather have you prophesy." So if you don't believe in speaking in tongues, then tongues is obviously not one of your gifts. You have to have faith and believe that God wants you to have a gift to receive it, I believe. But then again, if God wants you to have a gift, by golly, you're going to receive it. Jonah tried to run from his gift and look where it landed him—in the belly of a whale until he decided he wanted to do God's will. Yep, God has his ways to get through to us.

I believe you need to be open for whatever God wants to do in your life. Why do you think there are so many denominations of churches? I believe it is because of people's *opinions*. One believes this and the other that. So ones with different opinions go out and create a denomination that fits their style. Am I wrong?

But what is the *one* thing we have in common? It should be that Jesus Christ was the only begotten Son of the Father God and died on the cross for everyone who believes in his heart that he did this and rose from the dead three days later and sits at the right hand side of God. Am I wrong? No! *Opinions* separate churches, and therefore we do not have full unity—that is the only prayer we can answer for Jesus, with God's help, of course. We could have unity, but opinions are separating us.

The enemy prowls around like a lion, and unity will never happen with man's strength but only with God's. John 17:20–23 says:

> My prayer is not for them alone. I pray also for those who will believe in me through their message, that all of them may be in one, Father, just as you are in me and I am in you. May they also be in us so that the world may believe that you have sent me. I have given them the glory that you gave me, that they may be one as we are one: I in them and you in me. May they be brought to *complete unity* to let the world know that you sent me and have loved them even as you have loved me.

Here is a question. How many Holy Bibles are there? I mean, are there different Bibles for all the different denominations? No! There are different translations, but they all should be saying the same thing, but just in different words. So it is a little easier to understand. For the King James version is hard for many to understand, so this is why we have the different translations. Do we all go by the Ten Commandments? We should. But does one denomination have seven commandments or five? No!

If you can back your theory with the Holy Bible, and it plainly states and sides with your theory, then I will believe it. Some religions base their beliefs on the Bible, but only parts that go well and support *their* own theories. So, are these *theories* from the *evil one?* I would have to say yes, to bring God's children away from unity and into confusion.

Arguing about our differences is useless. Someone ends up walking away upset. If you don't believe that God still distributes gifts of the spirit, then more than likely, you won't experience the gifts. Don't put God into a bottle and break him out whenever you think you need to. Pray and be open to his gifts. You just might be blown away on how long you have been deceived to believe he doesn't perform miracles anymore or distribute gifts of the Spirit. You just might be able to witness to others who believe what you used to believe. Look at Paul. He hated and persecuted God's people but then ended up being one of God's greatest apostles.

Bottom line, folks: How can you say you hate sourdough bread if you haven't tried it? Then how can you tell a person who has experienced a miracle or a spiritual gift from God that you don't believe in them?

I'm not trying to push anyone into believing something they have never believed, but be open to God's gifts and pray that if they are real that he would bring you your gifts. Remember, my gifts are not your gifts. You will have different ones than I do, or anyone has, for that matter. God will smile upon you and will bless you with the gifts he has planned for your life. He had them planned before you were even a thought, and the gifts he gives you will fit you like a special-made glove, just for you to glorify him. We will be able to do more if we quit spreading our non-biblical opinions around like a disease or wildfire. We just also might experience unity and see God work in ways that will blow our minds and theories away!

THE ABOVE LOVE

Don't you know?
Your life is God's show.
He records your every move.
There is only one thing to prove,
That you have love,
The kind that comes from above.
When there is love, you will not lack,
Or find yourself talking smack.
It's a peaceful, pure feeling.
Rewards in heaven you are sealing.
Whatever the cost,
Let pure love never be lost!

So many songs, books, and movies have been based on this one emotion. But how many of us exercise true love? Do you think not trusting stops us from truly pouring out the kind of love God wants us to? I believe it could be some of the problem. Do you truly love someone if you don't tell him or her the truth or hold him or her accountable for his or her actions and words? I don't believe we truly do love if we don't share the truth with one another.

God loved us so much that he gave his one and only Son, Jesus Christ, to die on a cross to forgive us of our sins, not his. John 3:16 says, "For God so loved the world that he gave his one and only Son, that whoever believes in him shall not perish but have eternal life." God looks at us through Jesus. He doesn't see your sin if you've asked for forgiveness through his Son. Jesus took all of our sins upon himself so God the Father would look at you and me through Jesus, not directly at us. If God didn't send his only Son to intercede for us and basically be the middleman, we would be doomed.

The word *love,* in my opinion, is used way too broadly. True love has basically been missing in action since the devil had his fit. I hear people say, "I love ya, brother" and then turn around and stab that brother in the back or put some sort of curse on him with their words.

Faith and love have an ingredient to make them work—that is *exercising* them! You can't get anything without working for it. Have you ever had a bad day and hoped that someone would show you love with a compliment or affection of some sort? *Everyone* has! Yes, even us guys, no matter how tough we say we are.

We can pray until we are blue in the face for faith and love, which God has already blessed us with, but unless you *step out* in faith, how can God answer your prayers? What are you giving God to work with?

TOOLS FOR TRADES

As a hunter sits on a hill,
A collector sends out the bills.
Firemen put out fires
As electricians string out wire.
Cops stop crime,
As a poet types rhymes.
A carpenter hammers nails,
And a sailor puts up sails.
Fishermen use worms
As a lawyer seeks a firm.
There are tools for every trade.
Each has its purpose that God made!

Every trade has a tool and a purpose. Those tools used for specific trades cannot be used in any other trades. A lawyer can't drag a fire hose into court. Is that a tool used in the court of law (unless, of course, it's evidence)? Can you picture a tax collector bringing in a gun to the IRS office? Can you imagine a hunter bringing his computer and office phone into the great outdoors while hunting? Every trade has a tool and is used specifically for that trade, and most times, that tool cannot be used for any other job besides the one it was created for.

How many people quit reading the Bible and start reading books like this one, hoping to get their daily dose of spiritual uplift? Romans 10:17 says, "Consequently, faith comes from hearing the message, and the message is heard through the word of Christ." So it is the Bible where we get our faith and understanding of his word. This comes from going to church and/or Bible studies. People do get a spiritual lift out of reading books, but focus on the one that has all the answers. These kind of books will give you encouragement and a different point of view, but be careful. Don't get me wrong; I hope the good Lord is speaking to you left and right and you can't sleep tonight because of the great revelation reading this book.

Still, the Holy Bible is Jesus' testimony and holds the entire truth you and I will ever need to know. The Bible teaches us how to live our lives. There is only *one* tool for salvation and godly principles and that is the Holy Bible. Many want to get in touch with themselves spiritually and practice magic, sorcery, witchcraft, or whatever new age thing is popular at the time.

The only tool for us to live by is the Holy Bible. It

will teach you everything you need to know: how to raise a family, how to do business, and how to treat one another. The Bible teaches about everything under the sun. You won't find more words of wisdom anywhere. The Bible is the only master tool needed to help everyone live by right standards and the *only* tool needed to bring salvation to the lost. Books like these also help individuals. But remember like a master key fits any key hole, the Bible is the master key needed for salvation.

What tools do you use to guide your life? I hope it is the only tool that God the Father sent to us. The only book that has Jesus' true testimony of who he is—God's only Son who was sent to die on a cross for *everyone* that will believe and take the *free* gift of salvation. He's the only one that had no sin, who took the world's sin upon himself because there was no other way we can be pure in the Father's eyes.

So be careful of whom and what you listen to and what you read. Don't buy the tools from Satan claiming to connect you to yourself or any other spiritual thing. Run and get out of there fast! Satan is a sly, sneaky, lying, cheating, and a no-good thing that only wants people to join him in hell for eternity. Don't believe him!

FALSE SECURITY

Many live their lives through the TV,
Or when camping, use an RV.
It seems as if we can't live with-
out modern-day appliances.
Technology is where we have put our reliance.
This will be America's downfall.
It will bring us to our knees and a crawl.
We don't know what it's like to live without.
Our gadgets add up to a high count.
In the end,
It doesn't matter what we spend
Or the toys we have acquired.

For in the end, everything will be refined by fire. How many hours do you and your family watch TV per day? Whatever happened to the good old-fashioned kind of entertainment? So many Americans spend so much time in front of a TV that we seem to live out all our dreams through the TV. We can travel and go places without spending anything, except the thirty dollars for the cable bill a month. Whatever happened to adventure? Where have our morals gone?

What kind of programs do you watch on TV? Are they good, wholesome shows your kids can watch? Or do you watch shows with cursing and nudity or ones with violent plots? I hear so many Christians say, "You just can't get away from that stuff anymore. That stuff is in all shows." I'm well aware of the morals most producers have. But it is up to you on what you and your kids watch. You do have that power. Quit blaming the movie industry and our public school systems for what you are not doing for yourselves or your kids at home—teaching morals and standards and applying them.

I'm afraid our reliance on technology will be one of America's downfalls. An "instant society wants instant results." I can't remember where I heard this saying, but it couldn't be truer. How many of us have stood in front of a microwave impatiently waiting for that gross TV dinner to get done?

Now, if we have to wait a couple of minutes for anything, we are ready to go through the roof with impatience. We as a society have pretty much gotten anything we have wanted with a snap of the fingers, meaning it is easy for us to go to the stores here in America and get any kind of food we want. But across seas, they struggle every single day with starvation, thirst, diseases, and sanitary issues.

If we as Americans can't get whatever we want in an instant, we are irate or seem to think it is the end of the world. We want instant results whenever we want something. But I can see why we are this way. We are able to go out and have any kind of food or vehicle or house we want as long as we work for it. This is a *great* freedom that many of us have taken for granted, and I see why it appears to other countries that we are very spoiled. What do you think? Are we?

Most people in America would be lost and die without the simple invention of power. We count on power to heat and cool our homes and for cooking.

What do you think would happen if America lost its power plants? I believe it would have drastic effects on Americans. Most people would not know how to survive if this sort of thing happened. Would you know how to cook without power? Would you be able to hike if your vehicle was shut down and could not be started again? Would you know what to eat in your local forests? What would kill you or what would give you the nutrition to survive? My point is that we are too dependent on things that could be taken away in a second.

Do you share with others what he has blessed you with already? In the end, it doesn't matter what you had because it was never yours to begin with. It was God's. We will not take anything with us, not even the grave clothes we get buried in. You were born with nothing, and you will leave with nothing. So be generous with what God blessed you with. It does the soul so good to be able to give a helping hand to ones in need. Matthew 10:8 says, "Freely you have received, freely give." Luke 6:38 says, "Give, and it will be given to you. A good measure, pressed down, shaken together and running over, will be poured into your lap. For with the measure you use, it will be measured to you." What do these verses speak to you? Are you being generous? Are you putting your hope into false securities?

TOMORROW'S CHILD

As I hear the child cry,
I breathe in and let out a sigh.
I wonder to the Lord, *Will this child draw nigh?*
Or will he be deceived by the enemy's lies?
I pray the parents raise him to God's standards
And teach him his morals and manners.
What is in store for tomorrow's child?
In the Lamb's Book of Life, will his name be filed?
As the child weeps,
I pray the Lord his soul he keeps.
As the mother loves away the tears,
I pray the child's salvation be near.

Having children is a tough decision to make as the end days draw nearer. As I look around and see children playing, I can only wonder and imagine the trials and hard times they will see in their lifetime. I pray they only make the one most important decision in their life—to accept Jesus Christ as their Lord and Savior. The enemy has so many deceiving tricks and lies that all I can do is pray they get the truth and apply the truth. Here is a warning to those who cause a child to sin. Mark 9:42 says, "And if anyone causes one of these little ones, who believe in me to sin, it would be better for him to be thrown into the sea with a large millstone tied around his neck." I don't think I want that kind of necklace. The responsibility lies on the shoulders of the parents until children are old enough to make their own decisions. But how they are brought up will tell you of their outcome, to a certain extent.

I think, also, about the families already deceived and how the parents will bring up their children to follow their same traditions. Traditions will not lead to eternal life. So my hope for tomorrow's child is that the truth will come to him with strong conviction, which will hopefully lead to eternal life with the Father. As a baby weeps, I weep for the babies. We are all born with sin, but where do children learn how to apply sin? They mainly learn from the evil one, but also their role models, which could be parents, siblings, friends, or whomever they hang around the most.

Children have such a pure curiosity. When they ask questions, answer them and do not beat around the bush about the subjects. If children ask you a question, give them the truth because they have heard something from somewhere or seen something and they need to hear the truth from the parents, I believe. After all, if you do not answer their questions, someone else will and you might not like the reply they get. So which answer do you prefer your children get?

So what is in store for tomorrow's child? Only the Father knows and only time will tell. Every child needs prayer. Your prayer could be the only prayer that a child is receiving. Pray that the Lord is near at all times and their salvation is near. Pray their spirits receive the good news of salvation. Better yet, if you know the Lord, witness to that child instead of hoping someone else will! Shed a tear for all of tomorrow's children. For their lives are just beginning and they will have many hard decisions to make in their lives. Love will clear a child's tears, as the Father's love will clear yours away!

HOLY PROMISES

I'm only here for a little while.
That's enough to make me smile.
I only wait on time.
Then eternal life will be mine.
No more pain
Or doing things in vain.
I'll go where my hope will never die,
And I'll never hear another lie.
I'll be where God's angels are at a stance,
Ready to praise in advance.
Oh, Father, I cannot wait
For my eternal date!
But while I'm here,
Help me praise your name with reverence and fear.

Praise the Lord; we are only here for a little while. The longer I live, the more I respect my elders for living in a world that wears you down each and everyday. Life is tough. Sometimes I wonder how some people have the strength to be here on earth for so long. Sometimes life just seems to drag on. I think we all feel like this at one point or another in our lives.

But the longer I live, the more I appreciate the grace God has given me. Without it, I wouldn't be here. Before I knew the Lord as my Savior, I didn't care much about anything, except about myself and what pleased me. Now that I do know Jesus as my Savior, I can't see or even understand how I made it so long without him. Something that does make me smile is the only thing standing between my eternal destination and me is *time.* Think about it. Won't it be nice? No more pain or doing things in vain. No more lies or games. It will be nice!

But in order to experience the kingdom of heaven, you need to accept the free gift God offers to all right now, for tomorrow could be too late. That is the *free* gift of salvation. We cannot earn it! In heaven, our dreams will all come true; our hope will never die. Wow! Are you sold yet? Does heaven really need to be sold to anyone?

Most people believe that they are okay with God and that they will go to heaven. Do you follow the Ten Commandments? Do you bless people even when they curse you in your face? Do you hold people accountable for the things they do and say? Do you love the Lord your God more than your husband or wife or kids? You should! Matthew 10:37–38 says, "Anyone who loves his father or mother more than me is not worthy of me; anyone who loves his son or daughter more than me is not worthy of me; and anyone who does not take his cross and follow me is not worthy of me." Do you believe all these things to be true with all your heart, soul, and mind? More to my point, do you live these things out every day of your life to the best of your ability? You will never be perfect, but do try to apply biblical standards the best that you know how everyday. If we do not apply God's decrees, we will not see God's full blessings.

The most important thing is accepting Jesus as your Lord and Savior, and this is a free gift that can never be bought or worked for. Everything else you do in life will determine the rewards you will receive in heaven. Jeremiah 17:10 says, "I the Lord search the heart and examine the mind, to *reward* a man according to his conduct, according to what his deeds deserve." Matthew 16:27 says, "For the Son of Man is going to come in his Father's glory with his angels, and then he will reward each person according to what he has done." So, see, you will be rewarded when you make it to heaven according to what you do. But faith is what saves you.

While we are here on earth, store up treasures for yourself for the kingdom of heaven. Matthew 6:20–21 sums it up by saying, "But store up for yourselves treasures in Heaven, where moth and rust do not destroy, and where thieves do not break in and steal. For where your treasure is, there your heart will be also." Love will keep you on God's path. If you are easily angered and do not treat others the way you want to be treated, then whose path are you on? Praise God through everything, love your neighbor as yourself, and fear God, for the fear of God is the beginning of wisdom.

CHANCE BY DEATH

Praise Jesus; he gave me a chance,
So God wouldn't give my sins a second glance.
I can't give back what God freely gave.
I can't do enough, for my soul he saved.
Please, God, bring my fate,
For the zeal you gave me cannot wait.
Salvation only cost me my pride to ask,
A cheap price for life that will last.
Salvation cannot be earned,
But a gift that must be learned.

If you haven't got the hint yet, Jesus died on the cross for everyone's sins. If he hadn't done this, we, as Gentiles, would not have a chance for eternal life. The only reason why we have the chance now is because his people had hardened hearts and would not obey his commands. Because of their hearts, God went to a people that would obey and listen—the Gentiles.

Romans 11:25–32 says:

> I do not want you to be ignorant of this mystery, brothers, so that you may not be conceited: Israel has experienced a hardening in part until the full number of the Gentiles has come in. And so all Israel will be saved, as it is written: "The deliverer will come from Zion; he will turn Godlessness away from Jacob. And this is my covenant with them When I take away their sins."
>
> As far as the gospel is concerned, they are enemies on your account; but as far as election is concerned, they are loved on account of the patriarchs, for God's gifts and his call are irrevocable. Just as you who were at one time disobedient to God have now received mercy as a result of their disobedience, so they too have now become disobedient in order that they too may now receive mercy as a result of God's mercy to you. For God has bound all men over to disobedience so that he may have mercy on them all.

So only because of their disobedience, we received our mercy. But in the end, God will have mercy on all of his chosen children, the Jews. Since God gave Gentiles mercy, he will also give his children the mercy he gave us.

The old covenant really was for the people of God, the Jews. Because of their hardened hearts and much more, you and I have one chance to be redeemed through the blood of Christ Jesus. God will not take a second glance at our sins if we accept his Son as our Lord and Savior. It is a free gift, like I've said again and again, and we cannot do enough to earn his grace, for we already have it. The *only* cost for salvation is actually our pride.

The spirit of pride will make you or take you. Some of the signs of pride are always being right, not admitting even when you know you are wrong, not asking for help when it's needed, or not wanting to show anyone your weaknesses. I believe if you show you're human and have weaknesses, it shows your strength. No one wants to be around people who are always right and argumentative and prideful.

Some people believe they need every single fact before they accept Jesus as their Lord and Savior. To a certain extent, yes, you do need to know more about the denomination trying to get you to join their church. If we listen to man or woman and do not pay attention to the Holy Bible or the Holy Spirit, the road we take will be a dead end, and you will never know it until judgment day. The Bible and Jesus are the keys to your eternal success or failure.

The last sentence refers to learning the free gift of grace and salvation. What needs to be learned is what is in the Holy Bible, and that is it!

If someone is witnessing to you about a religion and

cannot back his theory in the Bible, do not accept it! Some religions use parts of the Bible or a few sentences from the Bible, but be careful; read the entire scripture to make sure you get the full meaning of what the Bible is trying to get across to you. Satan can come as a person wanting to help you. He doesn't come in a red suit and horns or with a pitchfork. He will come in as an innocent person wanting to deceive you down the wrong path.

Second Corinthians 11:13–15 says, "For such men are false apostles of Christ. And no wonder, for Satan himself masquerades as an angel of light. It is not surprising, then, if his servants masquerade as servants of righteousness. Their end will be what their actions deserve." Satan comes in many forms to deceive people. Follow your gut instincts—that is the Holy Spirit in you. Question them: "Are you a servant of Jesus Christ, the Lord and Savior of all?"

God does not change his covenants. His one and only Son, Jesus Christ's blood sealed the final covenant God has made for all who accepts him as Savior by faith! God's covenants remain the same now and forever. If they didn't, he would be a liar. That is impossible!

We need to have the kind of faith like we had when we were children. Remember that kind of faith? You just knew what you hoped for was going to happen and in most cases it did. The Bible sums up the kind of faith that we need. Mark 10:15 says, "I tell you the truth, anyone who will not receive the kingdom of God like a little child will never enter it." Have faith in God, and know he loves you. He sent his one and only Son Jesus Christ to die on the cross for your sins and mine, not his. There is no other way we can be saved. Check it out in the Bible.

Jesus is truly the place to put your faith—him and the Holy Bible, which is his testimony and his Father's.

VAIN BLESSINGS

God bless America
Seems to be the latest hysteria.
Are we blind?
Has God not been kind?
To get God's favor back,
Repent! And get on his track.
Do we deserve his favor
After our behavior?
Our deeds are worthless
And fruitless.
We give senseless justification,
Which leads to our frustration.
In the Bible are God's decrees,
Ones to take seriously and heed.
Grace for Gentiles is soon at an end.
Mercy, we will no longer be able to spend.
Wake up, pew warmers.
Don't end up as mourners.
Don't let another day pass,
For Jesus' arrival is coming fast!

Ever since September 11, 2001, I see signs everywhere saying, "God Bless America." I'm sorry, but this makes me a little sick to my stomach in the way that we, including myself, can't see God *has* blessed this nation more than any other. Our problem is we are never satisfied. As soon as we get something we want, we admire it for a little while, and then we move on to wanting something else. Are we idle?

How should God bless America? What else do we need? Hasn't God already blessed us with way more than our needs? Should God bless us with more adultery? More idolatry? Should he give us more blessings so we will turn our backs on him more than we already do?

Come on people, do you see the point I am trying to make? Why should God bless America more when we can't handle the blessings we have now? Every time we do something going against the decrees he has put in place for us, we are turning our backs on God. Those decrees were made and written so we would glorify his name, not our own, like we have been doing for the past few decades.

The more we take God out of this nation, the more trouble this nation will see. In my opinion, we are taking our freedom and our grace with God to a major breaking point. We are going through strong spiritual warfare, but some do not understand it or even want to acknowledge it. Like I said before, if we keep taking God out of this nation, he will leave and go bless another nation that will apply his decrees, not just talk them. He did it before when his own children's hearts were hardened. To this day, we see war and trouble in Israel.

Romans 11:11–12 says,

> Again I ask: Did they stumble so as to fall beyond recovery? Not at all! Rather, because of their transgression, salvation has come to the Gentiles to make Israel envious. But if their transgression means riches for the world, and their loss means riches for the Gentiles, how much greater riches will their fullness bring!

The Gentiles' time is soon running out. We have taken his blessings and mercy for granted way too long. If this nation does not turn from our ways, we will see more freak accidents, more drought, more fire, more diseases, more devastation in economy, and crashes in the stock market like we have never witnessed. Many will lose way more than ever before. If we repent, God will restore America so we can continue to do his will, but only for a little while longer. For the things happening now are in his Word. We can't get away from what must happen, but we could get more time. I believe if Americans would repent, we would see our land and our spirits restored.

America, count the blessings you have now and quit wanting more. God has blessed America! Now, America, bless *God!*

INTEGRITY

The word integrity should mean a higher quality of life. But so often I see the very opposite, even in fellow brothers and sisters in Christ. To me, this is very discouraging and confusing. If this is the way I feel, I can't imagine how God is feeling. Can we expect to continue to have favor with God if our integrity is as shallow as a kiddy pool? I know we all fall short of the glory of God, but we as believers are really exercising our grace with God on a daily basis. Just because we have been given grace does not mean we need to keep it in shape by exercising it. It means God forgave our sins, and because of that, we need to repent. Repent means to *quit* sinning and turn from your previous ways. Acts 3:19 says, "Repent, then, and turn to God, so that your sins may be wiped out, that times of refreshing may come from the Lord, and that he may send the Christ, who has been appointed for you—even Jesus." We need to be exercising repentance, not grace.

We have grown lazy in our ways and have taken God's favor for granted way too long. Look what happened to his people when they quit listening to God. He went to a people that would listen and follow his commandments. Those people were the Gentiles, known otherwise as you and me. Who else can God go to who will listen and follow his laws and decrees? Yep, you guessed it; no one else is left. Gentiles covers everybody. I know everything is happening for the purpose of God, but just maybe if we heed his warnings, he will give us more time. Time for what? Repentance, blessing others, witnessing, or whatever he has been placing into your heart for so long.

Do you keep putting off things until tomorrow or when the time is right for you? If you are living with this kind of attitude, I'm sorry to let you know, but God could demand your life away tonight or even right now. Then what? It will be too late for you to repent. The last chapter of your life could end in one second. You will not know when your time has come. So don't let the book of your life end in a way that you will regret for eternity. Just make sure to do your best and pray God has written your name in the Lamb's Book of Life!

If I came to your house and had permission to look at your computer, do you know I could tell what kind of integrity you have? I could check out what kind of Web sites you and your family have been on for the last few months, if not years. Did you know this? Do you log onto good Web sites? Ones that are wholesome and you wouldn't try to hurry and shut off if your spouse or kids came in?

Most people have the kind of integrity where they abide by God's laws in front of people, but in the privacy of their homes, they watch movies with all kinds of violence and sex and listen to music that promotes the same. You could be a good Christian at church and

Bible studies, but when you go home, what do you fill your mind with? There are a few examples of integrity. The first is the kind you put on in front of people. The second is your true integrity, the kind that you follow through within the privacy of your home. You also have the kind of integrity that you exhibit when you deal with others in business deals and while you work and play. Do you overpromise and under-deliver? Has anyone ever made you a promise and skipped out on it when it was time to pay up? Did that hurt you? Did you like it when that happened? Remember Matthew 7:12: "So in everything, do to others what you would have them do to you." How do you want others to treat you? Fairly? Then you treat them fairly.

In the year 2000, I worked for a well-known evangelist and author. He has written over fifteen successful books and has led many to the Lord. He has had the kind of success I hope for in my life, concerning the seeds of salvation he has planted in people's hearts. God has also given him great favor with important people around the world and so much more. I looked up to this man and really respected and loved him. But this man hurt me in such a way I'll never forget it.

Success has several different meanings to different kinds of people. One could be financial success; another is the kind that makes you feel good about what you do. For me, success is feeling my life is glorifying God. Still, I am human and mess up more than anyone. Continuing the story, when I worked for this man, he promised me lots of things and also his time. But those things never happened, and the time was an occasional talk at a local country restaurant. It was not the quantity of time spent, but the quality of time spent I was hoping for.

When I worked for this gentleman, I did construction or whatever he asked. I would run many errands, hire some people to do work, and basically was his personal assistant. He promised me overtime, which was never paid. He paid the normal time, but not the overtime. At that time I was struggling financially, so I asked him to take a little time out and help me create a budget. His advice was just to file for bankruptcy.

You can tell when someone really cares about you by the way they talk to you. Either they talk at you, which does not show love, or to you, which does show love. They also follow through on promises. Needless to say, I was not encouraged whatsoever by this man, but I continued to have hope. I can't begin to tell you how much I wanted to quit, but the Father told me to stay.

This man always suggested how others could help me, but he did not fulfill his promises. Instead, he gave me an overwhelming, burdensome load to carry. I put fourteen and sixteen-hour days in for this man. His repayment? Stealing (by not paying the overtime) and lying (not following through on a promise to go to pastoral school) to me. But come to find out, I was not the only one he was doing this to. Luke 11:46 says, "Jesus replied, 'And you experts in the law, woe to you, because you load people down with burdens they can hardly carry, and you yourselves will not lift one finger to help them.'"

After I spent six months working for him, the house was pretty much done. When I worked for him, this man would call me nearly every single day to check in with me about what was going on with his new home.

After I quit, I never heard from him again. Similarly, this man said thanks all the time, but his actions never lined up with his words. I was used and taken advantage of. He never followed through on any promises.

The Bible says not to take a fellow brother to court, so I didn't. I confronted this man with a fellow brother and sister in Christ on several issues. As usual, he talked himself right out of everything. His justification needed justified. Many people are wowed by his accomplishments. But I'm wowed at God's accomplishments through him!

For over a year, I held unforgiveness toward this man. After that, I couldn't take it anymore and wrote this man a five-page letter to confront him. That was the conviction I had. I gave the letter to him at Christmastime in church. When I did, I told him I loved him, and he said the same. The next week at church, I hoped for a time to talk, but when I saw him, I said hello, and he gave me a cold, cold stare. Then he turned his back on me, and cut me off, literally. I then knew his integrity.

It also took him some time to pay me the overtime, but like I stated before, he only paid me for the hours I worked and not the time and a half rate that gives the word overtime its meaning. I was also paid this check through my church. So it appears to me and others I talked to that he gave the church some of the money to pay me, but it shows as a tax write off for him, and he did not pay his taxes on payroll like he was supposed to.

I bring up this experience because it taught me so much. This man called me a son but didn't treat me like one. He took advantage of my heart and services. I now know his integrity; the truth will always shine through. He cared more about the house and what people could *do* for him than he did about the welfare of those he entrusted to do the quality work for him. Because of his behavior, he turned many people away from the gospel. I must say this man was consistent in one thing, which was being inconsistent.

Do not put any man or woman on a pedestal. He or she will always let you down in one way or another. The only one you can trust is the Father. He will *not* let you down. If he makes a promise, it will be kept at the time he sees fit to deliver. It's hard when you have been hurt so badly and you don't want to trust anyone.

But not everybody is the same, and not everybody forgets where he or she has come from, which is from the Father's grace. This man's actions and words hurt me so badly because I expected more out of a man that God so greatly anointed and uses. But after all, he is just a man like I am, and he is not Jesus. I thank God for the lessons learned and pray this man will quit doing things and stop and love people every now and then. I pray that God continues to give him favor, blessing him as he glorifies God and not himself. The name has been withheld for obvious reasons.

So integrity is dealt with every single day and in many shapes and forms. We need to go through hard times, for that is what builds our character. That is a way the Father will build your foundation so you won't blow over in the first windstorm. Your true integrity will show in the most difficult times of your life.

Do you realize if you have kids or if you just babysit, those kids are watching you very closely? Most often, what they see and hear you do, they will try and copy it. The first few years of a child's life are the years he or she learns the most. He or she will copy what you do and say and get the same basic temperament you have. Is your integrity the kind that you want your child to have?

Integrity will show up in your conversations, work ethics, business deals, and when you slam your fingers in the car door. Basically, your integrity will show up every single day in almost all of your activities. Integrity will witness to a nonbeliever or make him want nothing to do with you or religion.

So much is riding on your integrity. When claiming to be a Christian, your reputation is no longer your own, but the one you promote, *God.* Do you understand that what you do and say reflects your integrity? It can give you favor when you need it, or it could be the ruin of you. If you lose your integrity with people, it will take you years to get it back, if at all. Your integrity is the reflection of your spirit!

Remember, if you claim to be a Christian, people will watch you like a hawk to see if you will make mistakes. You will, because we all fall short of the glory of God. Even so, make sure you are attentive to the Holy Spirit, for the Spirit will guide you in your words and actions if you are listening. God has always been a gentleman. He will not push his way into your life. But he will speak to you with conviction, *not* condemnation. You know when your integrity glorifies God. For his spirit will reward you with great joy to let you know. Treat others as you want to be treated. Put yourself in their shoes. Do not talk God's words—exercise them!

DISCIPLINE

Life without discipline is a life of struggle. Proverbs 13:18 says, "He who ignores discipline comes to poverty and shame, but whoever heeds correction is honored." Most people believe discipline is punishment, but if we are not disciplined, what kind of world do you think we would be living in? When there is punishment, discipline must follow. Meaning, if a child went into a store and stole some candy and went back out to the car and his daddy caught him eating it, there would be punishment. The father needs to let them know what they did was morally wrong, so when they are punished they realize their actions will have consequences. Discipline will teach that child it is not right to steal candy, and hopefully, he will never do it again.

Although discipline is not enjoyable, it is needed to live a moral and healthy life. Discipline comes in many forms, and the above is only one example. Another example of discipline is going to work everyday. You need to have the discipline to go to bed at a reasonable hour the night before so you can wake up early the next morning and get to work on time. If you do not have this kind of discipline, you will be late, and eventually you will be fired because of your lack of discipline to show up on time.

Raising a family is a lot of responsibility. Without discipline, your children could end up in prison or join a gang and be dead in a week or two. Discipline is one of the most important ingredients to live a successful life, whatever your definition of success is.

Just as bread will not rise without yeast, you cannot live without discipline. Take world champion athletes for instance. They will not become world champions unless, first of all, they practice every single day at their sport to get good enough to compete professionally. Second, they need to travel and compete before they eventually make it to the world title event. Along the way, they need to put themselves into competition scrimmages to learn and deal with whatever problems could come up in real competitions. If they are not prepared, they will not win.

True champions are consistent with their discipline. That means eating healthy, practicing their style, working out, and basically doing whatever they need to do to win without cheating. Shortcuts will never work in the long run. If an athlete chooses to use any kind of drug to try and enhance his or her performance, eventually he or she will get caught or pay the ultimate price with his or her health. He or she might get by for a while, but it will catch up.

The slogan I wrote and quoted earlier, "Your discipline must be greater than the passion of your dream," rings so true to me. If you do not have the discipline to work toward your goals one step at a time, then all the passion in the world will do you no good. Passion is good; don't get me wrong, but if you lack the discipline to work toward those dreams, then that is all they are, just dreams. You will be going down a dead-end road. Do you believe an athlete who sits on the couch for a year eating pizza and Twinkies will go out and win a world title of any kind within the same year? Maybe a pizza-eating contest. Do you see how important discipline is? Without it, you cannot achieve much.

Most Christians want to live a spiritual life, but don't want to discipline themselves to live that spiritual life. We just put in a prayer every now and then and hope the good Lord will just drop the mother load into our laps. God can do that, but I believe he wants to do that to ones that are exercising their discipline and living as close to his Word as they can. If you put forth the effort, God will pour out his blessings on you so much that they will be chasing you down the street.

If you do not have discipline walking with God, that leaves an open door for the devil to sneak in and try to kill, steal, or destroy you. If you claim to be a Christian but don't have the discipline to live a Christian life, then it's not really a Christian life, is it? When I first gave my life to the Lord, I was living in sin. I slept with my girlfriend and did plenty of other stupid things. Later, when I really dedicated myself to God and his ways, I had to repent from what I was previously doing and discipline myself to follow God's way. Luke 13:3 says, "But unless you repent, you too will all perish." What do you think Jesus was talking about when he said this? He said this more than once.

Should we keep sinning once we know the truth when we know we have been given grace and forgiveness of sins? Let me be the first to tell you it was not easy for me to repent once I had already enjoyed pleasures of the flesh. The devil showed up more times than I care to talk about, trying to tempt me with women or whatever my flesh had a longing for. I must say, with God's strength, I have made it through and have been able to glorify God in many decisions.

When you decide to follow God, guess what? Yep, the devil will be right behind you to wait for *any* opening. He likes to use depression, condemnation, stress, moodiness, or any emotion at his disposal to get you off track. The discipline of being in the Word will teach you that you have the *authority* over Satan and all his attacks because of Jesus dying on the cross and shedding his blood. Colossians 2:9–10 says, "For in Christ all the fullness of the Deity lives in bodily form, and you have been given fullness in Christ, who is the head over every power and authority." We cannot take a vacation away from discipline. If you think you can, you will be fighting a spiritual war that could drain you. I wish the Lord would open everyone's spiritual eyes to see the battle being fought for them. The battle was already won when Jesus was raised from the dead, but the spiritual war right now is for your soul!

See, the battle has been won, but we have to make the decision to accept Jesus as our Lord and Savior in order to go to the kingdom of heaven. Salvation is a free gift; you do not earn it. You need to believe with all your heart that Jesus died for you on that cross and was raised from the dead by God three days later. You need to accept this with childlike faith. Some don't believe in what they can't see. They claim they can't see God, so they don't believe in God. How foolish! God has created the earth and everything in it!

What other kinds of "things" do people need to see

in order to believe? Luke 18:17 says, "I tell you the truth, anyone who will not receive the kingdom of God like a little child will never enter it." So if you do not have that childlike faith in God and his kingdom, you will *never* enter it. All it takes is for you to accept it. But what you do on earth will determine the rewards you will have in heaven.

Again, if you do not have discipline to learn what the truth is in the Bible, then you're cutting yourself short at your eternal expense. Books like this will be able to speak to you about subjects we go through today in this time, but the Holy Bible is the only book with the whole truth for today and forever! If you want to live a life to glorify God, then discipline yourself in the Word and know how to use the Word for your advantage. If you don't discipline yourself in this area, then life will not be a fulfilled one.

A spirit-led life takes the same kind of discipline that a champion needs to win. Discipline will come into every aspect of life, but it is up to us how much discipline we use to get to where we want to go. How badly you want to achieve something will determine the measure of discipline you will use in your life to get there. If you don't achieve your goals, did you honestly have enough discipline? Or did you apply just enough to get through whatever you needed to get through at the time?

Some people do discipline themselves very well and still do not achieve their goals. I can only say that persistence will beat the resistance, but some just do not put enough *time* into their goals to see them through as well.

Instant society wants instant results. If we have to

wait more than five minutes for a pizza to cook in a microwave, we are pacing the kitchen, fretting that we will miss our hot date or appointment. But if we had discipline, we would make sure to plan ahead and make sure there was enough time to grab something to eat.

Living a Christian life takes more discipline than one working toward a world championship. I'm talking about following God's Word as much and as close as you can. Temptations will come, but if we have been disciplined in God's Word, we will overcome anything that comes our way. It is not our strength that gets us through the tough times, but the Father's strength that will get us through anything. Practice what you preach. Discipline yourselves to follow through on God's Word. Your life is not a movie, and you won't have a director come in and say, "Cut, that's a wrap!" When the director does come next time, it will be to separate his sheep from the goats. Then you will find out where you will be spending eternity—heaven or hell. Discipline is the essence of what we will accomplish in life!

WITNESSING

Do you realize your actions witness to people more than your words? Proverbs 20:11 says, "Even a child is known by his actions, by whether his conduct is pure and right." When you witness to a nonbeliever, he will watch every move you make closely to see if you practice what you preach. Nonbelievers tend to wait for a time when you mess up just to rub it in your face that you are a hypocrite. To tell you the truth, I can't blame them. I've met some so-called Christians these last few years that would turn me away from God. Some claim to be Christians, but the only time they are Christians is at church and Bible studies. When they work, some treat their co-workers terribly. They curse like it was going out of style and join in on smack talking (gossip) like they never knew who Jesus was.

These people are supposed to be brothers and sisters in Christ! I can't stand it. With friends like these, who needs enemies? They are rude and only looking out for number one—themselves. Where in the Bible does it say this is how we are to act? I must not have the same Bible they have. This kind of self-righteous attitude will not point a lost soul toward God, but send him packing the other way. Can you live with that?

The truth here is these Christians are purely living in the flesh, not for God. They might be saved, but the way they live their lives is not a testimony to our Savior. Salvation is a *free* gift of grace from your loving Father God. Apply your Christianity. The Father knows all, and you will not make it by faking it!

Do you realize Satan uses believers as much as non-believers? You are doing his work when you put other people down, talk gossip, act rude, or do something that does not glorify God. Words like these are also known as curses. You tell someone he is dumb enough times, he will start to believe it. You might not want to be doing Satan's work, but you are if you do things like this.

How you behave also witnesses to people. If you're upset or angry and you stomp out of a room in front of others, you are witnessing. Your tone of voice witnesses to people, along with the way you project your words. Do you realize this? Almost every part of you, whether in tone of voice, projection of words, body language, or actions, is witnessing to someone. What do you want to witness?

Business people, you witness when you make a promise with your mouth and do not follow through on your word. I'm also a businessman, and I listen like a hawk to others to sense their integrity. If I get a bad feeling in my gut, we won't be doing business. Business people these days need to contact their lawyers before they can even talk business, it seems. Good character is so very hard to find in people, even in fellow brothers and sisters. It is ridiculous what we have to do today to protect ourselves. So many people have so many walls built around their hearts because of the fear of getting hurt or used.

We as believers are no better than nonbelievers at practicing what we preach. I find most nonbelievers are more honest than we believers are. What is wrong with this picture? I know it sounds like I'm going off on a tangent, but these are things the Lord has convicted me to write. Have you ever thought about these things or these points of views? This has also been my experience since I've given my life to the Lord. Then again, do not get me wrong. Not all brothers and sisters are like this, and I know ones that do follow the word as close as they can. I'm also no saint. We *all* fall short of the glory of God.

My point is that we all need to try a lot harder with what we do or say because it is witnessing to someone. If we can't give an encouraging word, then we need to keep our pie holes shut until something positive can come out. I'm not one to beat around a bush. I pray for boldness, and by golly, God is hearing my prayers.

Brothers and sisters, just take your time before you say something or do something. If it will not glorify God, then don't do it. My mouth gets me into many problems, so I know how hard it is. Jesus also knows how hard it is because he was here himself and went through more trials than you or I ever will. He also knows firsthand the temptations Satan will use to deceive us because he went through the same sort of things and worse. If you truly want to witness, live a life that is witness worthy. That goes with the things you say and do.

Whether in a business deal or making promises

to your employees, do not overpromise and then turn around and underdeliver. Treat and do things to others that you want done to yourself. Matthew 7:12 says exactly this, "So in everything, do to others what you would have them do to you, for this sums up the Law and the Prophets."

Selfishness is another problem we have today. Matthew 10:39 says, "Whoever finds his life will lose it, and whoever loses his life for my sake will find it." Whenever you get selfish and want things for yourself, you generally won't get what you want. On the other hand, if you go out, bless others, and pray for them, it is amazing how God will deliver exactly what you need at the exact time that you need it.

Go out and bless people; witness with a kind word or actions. Don't count on someone else to witness to your family or friends or co-workers, because today could be their last day here on earth. When Jesus lives in someone's heart, you *will* see change in that person's life. Literally, you will see changes in their attitude, who they hang around, where they hang out, their language, and everything you knew of them will generally change.

When someone truly knows Jesus as their Lord and Savior, he or she can't help becoming more like Jesus. Jesus didn't curse or lose his temper or get rude with people. He showed love. If you are saved and claim to know Jesus, then why are you still carrying on like a fool? *Ouch!* That will offend a few people because it's the truth. Revelation 3:15–16 says, "I know your deeds, that you are neither cold nor hot. I wish you were either one or the other! So because you are lukewarm—neither hot nor cold—I am about to spit you out of my mouth." Okay, people, if you are claiming to be a Christian, then you need to live like a Christian. There is no in between. Either you are hot or cold. (Cold, if I understand this scripture, will not be making it to heaven.) If you are witnessing, then let the life you live witness more than the words you speak!

UNITY

What is the one thing all Christians have in common? I will answer this question at the end of this chapter.

When praying one night, I had a question for God and that question was, "Why are there so many different denominations of Christianity?" As I sat there, I kept hearing the word *opinions* in my heart. After contemplating that word, it hit me like a holy brick across the head.

If you think about it, opinions separate the unity that the body of Christ should have, needs to have, and the unity God wants his people to have. As I talk with some fellow Christians about why they go to the church they do, I get many different answers. But the truth is they go to the church they go to because that is where they feel at home and comfortable. That is the truth, but I do not ever hear that.

I hear things like, "Oh, some Christians depend on the Bible too much and take it too literally!" Or, "That church believes in speaking in tongues, and I don't believe that happens today. That was just in the Old Testament they spoke in tongues!" Or, "People dance around in that church and raise their hands!" Or, "That church believes in miracles and prays for the sick, believing they will be healed. It's just too much for me, and it makes me uncomfortable!" Or, "When I walk into some churches, it seems so dead. No Holy Spirit!" Or, "They sing the same old hymns every Sunday!" Or, "The worship is so dead; it's not alive." Or, "It is too loud!"

Do any of these excuses sound familiar? Maybe you have used one of these a time or two. Are these excuses biblical? Or are these excuses actually your opinion? Let's start off with taking the Bible literally. What? How can you not take the Bible literally? The problem is too many Christians are too comfortable in their walk with God. If we do not take the Bible seriously, what then should we take seriously? Should we take all the new age spirituality stuff seriously? Should we 'tune' into our spirits and others?

Have you heard of some of the things people believe today? How many of you Christians read your horoscope everyday? Then you say, "Oh, I don't believe in that junk; it is just entertaining." What? Just entertaining? People, when you read trash like that, you are planting a seed into your mind and room for Satan to work! Is that what you want? More battles? How many of you Christians do the spiritual part of yoga? If you do these kinds of things, then that is exactly what you are doing—giving Satan a personal, handwritten invitation to mess in your life! Then when the battles get too bad and you can't take it anymore, you call out to God and ask for help. He will help, but you just put yourself through so much that didn't need to happen. During the time you wasted, God could have been using you to glorify his name.

The truth is if we do not learn the hard way, we just won't learn. Our family and friends warn us, but it goes right through the ears, past the brain, doesn't even stop to check in, and checks right out. People, the Bible is God's Word and the only words that we are to take very literally because we will be judged according to how much of that book we lived by.

Now let's talk about speaking in tongues. Either you believe in it or you don't! But do not tell the ones that have experienced this gift from God that it is not true. That is like telling a zebra he doesn't have stripes or a tail! In the first place, that zebra knows you're blowing a lot of hot air at him. Second, it's a waste of your time to tell that zebra such a thing because he *knows* what he has. So why argue about the subject? Tongues are a gift from God according to his Word.

If you do not possess this gift, then you have received other gifts from God. Let's find out what the Bible has to say about speaking in tongues. I am not going to quote these following scriptures for you, but I will list them. That way, you know these scriptures are in your Bible and you get some personal time with God in his Word. I will start off with 1 Corinthians 12:1–31. I want you to read all these verses so you will have more understanding of the full scripture and not just one or two verses.

Next, I want you to read 1 Corinthians 13:1–13. After you have read these scriptures, go to 1 Corinthians 14:1–40. The last part of this scripture seems to be what turns many people off. Granted, some spirit-filled Christians do not do things in a fitting or orderly way. Some will pop off speaking in tongues where they should not be speaking in tongues. A favorite part of these scriptures of mine says it best in 1 Corinthians 14:23: "Some who do not understand or some unbelievers come in, will they not say that you are out of your mind?" So ones that do have this gift need to be sensitive to how a non-believer would take speaking in tongues. If they have never heard it, it could make them run the other way.

Christians want to share the gifts God gives them, but sometimes they misrepresent God by saying, "Speaking in tongues is natural." If a new believer does not receive the gift, most often, he will question his faith and get frustrated. So please, be sensitive around nonbelievers or new believers. There is a time and place for everything. If God intends them to have this gift, then it will be God that gives the gift, not you. Tongues is a language between you and God. It is a personal prayer from your spirit. Tongues can also benefit believers if there is an interpreter. God can reveal things to you through the interpreter. When you are around fellow brothers and sisters who also have this gift, then speak away, but please use discernment!

Now, let's go to the subject of some church members dancing around, raising their hands, worshipping God. When I first gave my life to the Lord, I attended a few churches like this. At first, I thought people were a little nutty, and it almost turned me off. Some were doing what looked like the funky chicken dance. I prayed to God about this and asked him to speak to my heart if this was right or wrong. He gave a few scriptures on the subject. Psalm 29:11 says, "You turned my wailing into dancing." Psalm 149:3 says, "Let them praise his name with dancing and make music to him with tambourine and harp."

God spoke to my heart, and it made perfect sense.

He said, "Why are you judging how my children worship me? Do not worry what other people do. Find your own way of worshipping me." God cares more about what is going on in that heart of ours more than he cares if you dance or raise your paws in the air. When I see people dancing before the Lord, it now gives me great joy. That is not my personality, but I do raise my hands every now and then. So you worship God the way you worship him, and quit worrying about how others do it. Sometimes it does get distracting how some people worship, but you focus in on God, not how everybody else does.

Now, about the gift of laying hands on the sick and praying for God to heal them. I went to a church a couple of years ago and the pastor was giving a message about how he didn't believe God does miracles anymore and miracles only happened in the early church. He made a comment about if there was anybody in the congregation who believed they could heal the sick, to come get him after the service and they would go to the hospital and see how many people would be healed. I was fuming! The key word he used was *they,* and it is not you or me who heals, but *God* does the healing!

God uses people who will *believe* in his gifts and sometimes uses ones who do not believe so he can use them as a testimony on his power. Look at Paul. He persecuted and killed God's people. Then he was touched by God and became one of the most successful apostles.

I met that pastor at the door with God's scripture to prove him wrong. He must have seen the fire in my eyes. He asked me to wait until he said good-bye to a few members, and he would get back to me. I waited for two hours for that man. He kept putting me off, even when every single member of that church went home. He left, and needless to say, I've never been back there. It wasn't my opinion that separated my unity with that church, but he did not speak biblically in his sermon. He spoke his *opinion.* The members were right behind him saying, "Amen, brother!" How many miracles do you believe this church sees? I hope God gives them many, so this man will be put back into his place.

Open up your Bible and go to Mark 16:15. Again, I will not quote it; I want you to see the words in your Bible. A part of this scripture says, "And these signs *will* accompany those who believe." It says *will,* not "maybe" or "might" or "this only happened in the Old Testament days." I also would like you to go back and read the scripture in 1 Corinthians that I gave earlier. If you can't remember what it said, it spoke several times about healing and laying hands on the sick. Come on, people! Read the Word and pray for insight and understanding of the Word. God will do it!

God will use people to lay their hands on sick people, and *he* will heal them because of the faith and belief of the ones receiving, praying, and/or if it is even God's will. *God* heals, not you or me! Healing is very much scriptural and in the Holy Bible. So why don't all Christians believe it still can be done? Because they are being deceived by others' opinions and by Satan himself. Satan doesn't want anyone to be healed, for it glorifies God.

A major problem with many Christians, in my opinion, is the fact that people just want to be comfortable. This reminds me of some scripture I've used before. Revelation 3:15: "I know your deeds, that you are neither cold nor hot. I wish you were either one or the other!" I believe being comfortable is being lukewarm. In the very next verse, 16, it says, "So, because you are lukewarm—neither hot nor cold—I am about to spit you out of my mouth." Get hot for God, people! He is hot for you! He sent his one and only Son to die on a cross for you. Get off the fence and live a life worthy for Jesus and what he did for us!

Don't get too comfortable. God just might want to do more in your life and ask some things from you that you never thought possible. Be open for what God wants to do in your life! Don't limit God. He doesn't limit you! The words in the Holy Bible are what we are to go by. God's Word has power; we have his strength in our weakness. Which would you prefer to live in, his strength or your weakness? Which would get you farther?

So when we decide on what church to be a part of, it all comes down to where we feel at home and comfortable. Some will walk into a church and see people dancing around and raising their hands. If they are not used to this or have never experienced this, they more than likely will leave and attend a church that is more traditional. There is nothing wrong with their decision! Not everyone has to worship or do whatever everybody else is doing. You need to attend a church that when you come out after each service, you should have learned, been challenged, and been touched somehow every time. If you attend a church where you are constantly looking at your watch to see if your pastor's hour is up, then I have two suggestions. Check your spiritual heart to see if you have grown lukewarm or cold. If not lukewarm or cold, then consider attending a different church.

If you're not growing in your relationship with God and learning more about the scriptures, then your time is basically time given to God in *vain.* If your heart is not worshiping God, you are more than likely just doing your *time.* This is wrong. God's Word has power and is alive. If the Word is not alive where you attend, then you need a godly awakening.

Some people say they don't like churches because of the worship music or that it is too loud. This matter is preference and opinion. These kinds of opinions should *not* separate the unity in God's churches, but they do. Some people say some churches are way too extreme. That depends on who they are comparing extreme to. Themselves? Then what they see could be extreme. But do not judge what and how others worship and praise God. Worry about what is going on inside of your own heart!

I have yet to find scripture that says you can't worship God while sitting in your pew or dancing before the Lord and raising hands to him is wrong. I have, however, found scriptures to *support* dancing and raising of the hands to the Father. Don't let these types of expressions separate us. When there is unity, there are numbers. When there are numbers, there is power—God's power!

I believe the main reason we do not have or experience God's kind of unity is because of our pride. The spirit of pride can destroy your walk with God, your family, relationships, your business, or anything you put your hands to. This spirit is always right and does not need any help. Pride always has everything under control. It also has a strong reputation of judging others. In reality, pride has nothing under control and over time will bring a person down to destruction if there is no repentance. For many centuries, pride has divided the unity God wants us to have. Remember, pride is always right, so each denomination believes it holds the truth and no one else does.

So are we living in truth, or do we even have the truth if we are judging each denomination? Some denominations do not hold the truth and are cults. So before you believe what someone is telling you, get into the Holy Bible and find out the truth for yourself. Some cults will use parts of the Bible, so be careful. Continually ask God to reveal the truth to you, and he will. Most experienced Christians will tell you to follow your gut instinct. That gut instinct is the Holy Spirit in us all. He will guide you to his truths and let you know when something is wrong. When you feel that faint emotion or feeling of conviction, do not confuse it with Satan's sense of condemnation. When making decisions, or anytime, bind up and rebuke the spirit of pride and cast it back to the pits of hell where it belongs. Remember Matthew 16:19: "I will give you the keys of the kingdom of heaven; whatever you bind on earth will be bound in heaven, and whatever you loose on earth will be loosed in heaven."

To answer the question from the beginning of this chapter, "What is the one thing that all Christians have in common?" That one thing is not a thing, but a person, Jesus Christ! Not only do Christians have this one person in common, but also anyone who will believe in Jesus and what he did has this person in common! Thanks to God's grace, he sent his only begotten Son to us, and Jesus, the only one without sin, took all of the world's sin so that we may have eternal life with him in the kingdom of heaven! Only by God's grace have we been saved. This is a free gift, and all it takes for anyone to get it is to accept Jesus as their Lord and Savior! Drop the pride, accept this gift before the book of your life is closed. No one knows when their last chapter is being written!

After all, *most* churches base their religion on this one man.

When there is unity, there is God's power. In God's power, things get done! Drop your opinions and stick to the known truth, Jesus Christ and the Bible!

CONVICTION OR CONDEMNATION?

God blessed each and every person with the gift of a free will. So that means we have the choice to ignore God's conviction. God is a true gentleman and will not force his way into your life. We have to yield to that faint inner whisper you hear. If you ignore the conviction, it will go away.

Our flesh can and will override our ability to make wise and discerning decisions. Oftentimes, after people shun God's conviction, Satan will come with condemnation. Your conscience knows when you go against God's will. Guilt tends to settle in and that is a sure sign condemnation will follow for some people. What I mean by *some* people is some people know God's Word and also are disciplined in obeying God's Word. In turn, they know they have full authority over the devil and his schemes.

But condemnation still sneaks into people's lives who are well disciplined. Condemnation does not discriminate. The devil will not string up a colorful banner in the front of your house to let you know he is launching an attack against you. Attacks from Satan will sneak in so delicately, and they are so well planned. If you are not disciplined in the Word, it could bring you to ruin.

Attacks can come in by fellow believers, family, circumstances, or any area Satan knows you struggle with. Matthew 7:13–14 says, “Enter through the narrow gate. For wide is the gate and broad is the road that leads to destruction, and many enter through it. But small is the gate and narrow the road that leads to life, and only a few find it.” Conviction is so important in our lives. If you heed God’s conviction, then you will be in his will. If you ignore his conviction, then the part of the verse that states, “For wide is the gate and broad is the road that leads to destruction, and many enter through it” means that you are choosing a path that seems to be the easiest and more of what your flesh wants and not what your spirit needs.

Scripture says many will enter through the wrong gate, and only a few will find the straight and narrow gate that leads to life. What does this scripture speak to your heart? Should you still be committing adultery or idolatry or hold un-forgiveness or continue to do what your flesh wants you to do? If you continue to do things your way, you will go through the gate that leads you to eternal punishment.

God sends his conviction to help us lead a righteous life, but it is up to you to heed and obey that conviction. How can we not take the Bible literally? If we don’t, we are testing God to see what kind of God he is, which you do not want to do. Meaning, I hear many people say they are fine with God, but continue to live very unrighteous lives. So they are testing God in the way if he will send them to hell. Do not test God, for you now have your warning if you haven't taken the rest of the warnings he has sent you!

God has given everybody more than enough chances to repent. He gave us his Son, his Word, and his spirit to help us lead the kind of life he wants us to live. What else do we need? God loves each and every person. If you choose to take the easy life and do what pleases you and not God, then I'm willing to bet the road your taking is the broad one. That road only leads to destruction!

So the bottom line is conviction is as important as God's Word itself. It does not take a genius to figure out when we are living in sin. The conviction tells you so. Conviction is a whisper from God. Condemnation is an overwhelming guilt, which will hold you in bondage with the devil until you wake up and kick him out of your life.

We all have a tug of war going on in our lives. One side wants you to make righteous decisions and the other wants to please your five senses: what feels good, what looks good, what tastes good, what sounds good, and what smells good. Do not live by your five senses; that will lead you into sin! Pleasing the senses could cost you your soul. Let your conscience be free of sin and guilt. Heed that faint whisper of conviction speaking to your heart and take action! A free conscience is a free spirit to do God's will.

VOWS

Have you ever made a vow to God? If yes, have you kept your vows? God hears all your promises and knows the desires of your heart. He knows the rash promises you do not intend to keep and the ones you do. Many times, we will make vows intending to keep them. When hard times come, however, we forget those vows we made to others and to God. Instead, we follow what our flesh wants and not what God wants. Most of us seem to think running away from our problems will solve everything. In reality, running away causes more pain for everyone involved.

Let's take marriage for instance. When you marry, you make vows to each other and to God. But many are not willing to see those vows fulfilled. One of the main reasons, I believe, is because of the lack of communication. At the beginning of relationships, you would do anything for each other. In the beginning, guys listen to their girlfriends' needs, bring them flowers, and go out of their way to bring them joy.

Women at the beginning of relationships also do things to bless their boyfriends. In time, we start to take each other for granted and those simple gestures each other used to do for the other. We get comfortable in our relationships and expect everything to be peachy without doing any maintenance or exercise for the fitness of the relationship.

The same goes regarding our walk with Jesus. We do not want to put forth any effort, but we expect God to continue to bring his blessings to us. We no longer go out of our way to bless others, but expect others to keep blessing us. If you want someone to bless you, bless them, let them know you appreciate them and love them. Do not expect repayment. Try to do things with love and as a blessing. In return, you will be storing treasures in heaven for yourself.

People you bless will see your compassion for them and feel your love. Just maybe they will remember what you did for them, and just maybe that love you showed them will rub off and bless someone else in need. How much more does this apply to your spouse? To fulfill marriage vows, it will take two. Not fifty-fifty, but one hundred-one hundred! Being one-sided will only make the other resent the relationship. Then things will be done in vain and not out of love. As you can see, the vows you make to each other and to God will take effort.

Now that we have made some common-sense observations, let's see what God has to say in his Word about vows. Numbers 30:2 says, "When a man makes a vow to the Lord or takes an oath to obligate himself by a pledge, he must not break his word but must do everything he said." The following passages talk about vows that a woman makes. To sum it up, it says that if a girl makes a vow, she is held to it unless her father hears about it. If he does not agree with the vow, he can nullify it. The Lord will *not* hold that girl to her vow. But if the father says nothing to her and knows about the vow, she is held to it.

The same applies to a woman who marries. If the husband does not agree with the vow, he can nullify it and the Lord will not hold her to it. However, if the husband says nothing and knows about the vow, she is held to it. If the man nullifies a vow, the guilt will be on him. Divorced women and widows do not have this out. Their vows are binding.

That pretty much wraps up what the rest of this section of scripture talks about for the vows women make. Any vow a man makes to God is binding on him. The New Testament backs this up. Matthew 5:33 says, "Again, you have heard that it was said to the people long ago, 'Do not break your oath, but keep the oaths you have made to the Lord.'" According to scripture, we had better fulfill our vows and oaths. If you cannot remember if you have made a vow, pray and ask God to bring the memory back so you can fulfill it. You might forget, but God will not.

Divorce is such a touchy subject for some, probably because they have been through one or their parents have been through one. Marriage seems to be one of the most common vows broken to God and to each other. When is divorce okay? What does God have to say about divorce? Matthew 19:9 says, "I tell you that anyone who divorces his wife, except for marital unfaithfulness, and marries another woman commits adultery." One mistake generally leads to several life-altering circumstances. For the adulterer, that few minutes of fleshly pleasure takes away a family, home, trust, love, possibly a career, and it could go on and on. For those who are guilty of this, would you still make that life-altering mistake if you could go back? I don't care what your pride says; I do not believe you would.

Coming from a divorced family, I can say that when parents divorce, their children will also divorce a part of their parents. Think about that for a minute; there is no explanation to that statement, but just truth. Kids more or less have a spiritual divorce, in my opinion, when parents divorce. Keep your vows to your partners. Communicate with each other. Neither one of you is perfect, so quit expecting your spouse to be! In divorce, you're not only divorcing your spouse, but also your blessings! It all depends on what you feel your blessings are.

I would like to take some classic history of broken vows. I would like to pay tribute to the Native American Indian, all tribes. Native Americans are the true Americans, in my opinion. History tells me that Christopher Columbus discovered America, or the land, but how could he find America if the Native Americans were already cooking his goose over their campfire? Old Chris just found the land already inhabited. Native Americans were already living in America for centuries.

When white people came to America, they brought nothing but heartache and despair for these people. They brought disease and war. White men made more promises to the Native Americans than there are needles on a pine tree. Rarely were any promises kept to these people. Vows to all tribes were nothing but empty words. I'm not saying Native Americans were perfect, but my point is we treated these people the way we did, in my opinion, to only get the land. We put them on reservations and told them they couldn't cross lines after centuries of roaming the land as free people.

These promises made are like some of the promises we make to God—hollow promises to only get what we want and to advance our plans, not God's.

One's integrity shines through when a promise is made and kept. One who does not follow through is usually not a person you would want to do business with. Native Americans did not give up hope for someone to follow through on what they kept promising. Treaty after treaty, promise after promise, was broken by *both* parties, but many rode on the shoulders of the white man.

Native Americans have reaped punishment for ill-gotten gain, white man's gain. Ever hear "Actions speak louder than words" before? Promises are empty unless there is action behind them. Actions are the best way we can witness. If you say, "I love you," then show them you love them. History has plainly shown us what broken vows are. What happened to the Native Americans is a prime example of vows not fulfilled. Don't let your vows be broken.

Concerning your vows, are you writing a big check on a closed account? The only way to keep an account open is to make periodic deposits. Are you making deposits of kept promises? When you are responsible with the little, God will give you bigger and better responsibilities. The same goes with vows. When you fulfill your promises, God will bless you even more. I believe he wants to bless people who will bless.

People seem to make a lot of promises to God when they are in trouble. Their prayers and petitions rise up to the Lord like smoke from a fire. He hears our requests, but he knew them before we ask. Sometimes in our prayers, we make vows like, "If you deliver the finances I need, I promise I'll tithe and bless others!"

The key word in that sentence is *if.* We need to tithe and offer and bless others even if God does not deliver the finances. When the times are tough, we need to forget about ourselves and bless others with what we have. If you're praying for finances, bless others financially. This kind of faith touches God in way that blessings from him will chase you down the street, beating you over the head. I can stand that kind of beating. Put yourself last, and your blessings will come. Some vows are empty and desperate to get what we want. But some are not, and God knows where your heart is. Pray and ask God if there are any vows you have forgotten. Do your best to fulfill them.

Some vows cannot be accomplished without God's help. They should not be on your shoulders, but his. So if your vow is too big for you to accomplish, it's okay, for it is not too big for God. He is the one who planted those hopes and dreams into your heart, and he wants to see them come to pass. The majority of the time, God waits on us to heed his ways before he delivers. If he didn't work this way, the blessings could become a burden. But his blessings will not be a burden because they won't come on your time. They will come on his appointed time, when your foundation is solid and able to handle the responsibilities.

If we don't fulfill our vows to God, having his help and strength already, how in the world can we expect to fulfill our vows to each other without his divine help? By God's grace and his strength is the only way we can fulfill *any* vows or our destiny. By not fulfilling vows or following God's laws and decrees, you will be looking at a business end of God's justice. When Jesus returns it will be to judge, not to have mercy. Salvation and mercy taken now will be sweet later. Hope for mercy when Jesus returns, without salvation, will only end in despair!

TEN COMMANDMENTS

The Ten Commandments are the highest standard of living by which we must live. The commandments are not laws from man, but from God himself. The laws God has put into place for us here on earth are not burdensome or hard to live by. The Ten Commandments cover every law there is, spiritual and man-made. Those ten rules will determine every person's fate. If they are followed, there will be eternal rewards; if they are not followed, there will be eternal consequences. Our lives here on earth are so short, but that short period of time will determine where you will spend your eternal time. By following God's law, you will follow all other laws. But in order for you to follow God's law, you need to understand them. To understand them, you need to be reading and meditating on God's Word, the Holy Bible. You also need to go to church and fellowship. There are many more of God's laws in the Bible. But again, the Ten Commandments cover everything.

I hear so many times about how people would rather go into the mountains to worship God instead of going to church. I love the great outdoors as much or more than anyone else, and I too once said I'm closer to

God in the mountains. Physical closeness will not get you the understanding of his Word and decrees. We need to have the *spiritual* closeness, the kind you get from praying and meditating on God's Word. Being around fellow believers will grow your faith and the understanding of God's laws in his Word. The mountains will give you peace for a while from being in the solitude. But when you're in the presence of God, there is healing, encouragement, and faith to move those wonderful mountains you're in, and God's peace will last an eternity.

When God has touched someone, you will see change in his or her life. The only way we will get touched by God is to seek him with all we have. Yes, you can do this in the mountains. But your understanding of God's principles, decrees, and faith comes from hearing the Word of God. Romans 10:17 says, "Consequently, faith comes from hearing the message, and the message is heard through the word of Christ," which is at church and the Bible! I just hope it does not take a tragedy before people turn to God for help. But sadly, that seems to be the only time many will start to pray and seek his ways and not their own. To know the Ten Commandments and God's full law is to study his Word, go to church, attend Bible studies, and fellowship with brothers and sisters in Christ; doing these things will give you the knowledge you need.

Some say they do not have the time to attend these kinds of functions. Then I say, "If you will not make the time for God, why should he make the time for you?" Remember God's promise in Matthew 18:19–20: "Again, I tell you that if two of you on earth agree about anything you ask for, it will be done for you by my Father in heaven. For where two or three come together in my name, there am I with them." When we come together as fellow believers, the power of God will be greater.

God hears your prayers on that mountain, but seriously, how much of your time are you meditating on God and his decrees? The majority of the time, when in the great outdoors, you are more worried about fishing, hunting, hiking, and basically whatever pleases you, not God. This statement may rub some people the wrong way, but it is the truth, and the truth will offend. In numbers, there is strength and God's power. You can enjoy God outside in his creation; after all, he made the earth for us to enjoy. Still, when you put yourself in church, you will grow, and his Word will become alive. No trophy hunt, hike, horseback ride, or fishing trip in the world can touch what you can experience in God's presence.

Mark 12:30–31 says, "Love the Lord your God with all your heart and with all your soul and with all your mind and with all your strength. The second is this: 'Love your neighbor as yourself.' There is no commandment greater than these." These words are quoted from Jesus himself. Do you realize that if we stood on these two commandments, we would be obeying the other commandments simply from obeying these two? Have you ever heard the saying, "Keep it simple, stupid?" I love this saying, and I have no idea who wrote it. It is just the truth, plain and straightforward.

We always want to complicate things. The Ten Commandments are simple and fairly easy to abide by, but when you get humans in the way is when things start to get complicated. Human nature tends to have an explanation for everything or wants to fix everything, and if there is no explanation or we can't fix it, we add loopholes into law, man's and God's.

Human nature is dangerous. If we start putting in extra words in God's law to suit our own desires and put our conscience at ease, we are writing a check we will not be able to cash. We will then have to answer to the president of the Life Eternal Bank. We will not like his prognosis and reaction, but it's not like we haven't been warned many times. Yet, we still keep doing what fits our needs. If we would only put God's needs first, ours would be more than met. But who here on earth has that kind of faith? Who here really thinks of themselves last? Some do, but not many!

God did not put the Ten Commandments into place to burden us, but to teach us the right way to live. How would we know if something was right if we are not told that it was right? God's law tells us exactly what is right and wrong. If God did not send us his Son and his Word, what kind of standards would we be living by? No one can answer that question, but you can pretty much come up with your own conclusion.

God gave us the tool to live by, his Word. How often you pick up that tool and use it is totally up to you. The more you pick it up and read it, the better you learn how to apply it. After you use it long enough, you will become a master at using that tool.

You can't expect to arrive at a construction site not knowing anything about construction and be able to use every single tool like a master carpenter, can you? It will take time for you to get the feel for every tool. Nevertheless, after a few years of practice, you will be a master carpenter.

In the same way, when you first give your life to the

Lord, expect to put some years into building a strong foundation on his Word and building a relationship with the Father. You will not learn everything there is to know about that tool, the Bible, ever. God's Word has a way of teaching a Bible scholar new things when they are eighty years old and have studied it since childhood. It will take you time to learn the Word. Pray for God's help in understanding the Word. He delights in children who want to follow his heart. He will use you greatly, even if you are just learning his ways.

When it comes down to the Ten Commandments and God's law, never let your guard down for one moment. The devil is here to kill, steal, and destroy. Do not give him a chance to steal anything from you, including your family. Use your sword, the Bible, and learn the Ten Commandments and God's law. Apply them, for through them you will achieve victories and win rewards. That tool, the Bible, is the only tool that God uses to send out the good news of salvation through his workers. How much of that book you apply to your life will determine your rewards and punishments on judgment day!

REPENTANCE

Repentance is the key to forgiveness. If you are a believer and have been living in sin, repentance will get you back into the presence of God. We should all know God's Word to the point of knowing what is right and wrong. Sometimes the flesh will take over, and when that happens, sin will be present. We all make excuses why we sin, we try and justify to others and ourselves, but will God buy your justification? I do not believe he will.

The problem is that our justification needs to be justified. This reminds me of scripture in Hebrews 5:11–14:

> We have much to say about this, but it is hard to explain because you are slow to learn. In fact, though by this time you ought to be teachers, you need someone to teach you the elementary truths of God's word all over again. You need milk, not solid food! Anyone who lives on milk, being still an infant, is not acquainted with the teaching about righteousness. But solid food is for the mature,

> who by *constant* use have trained themselves to distinguish good from evil.

Have you known the Lord for a while? Long enough to distinguish what is right and wrong? If you have known him for a while, then you have no excuses!

I'm not going to beat around the salvation bush. People, we have taken God for granted long enough. It is time to grow up! Get weaned off the milk, and let's start eating some steak! Did you hear me? Grow up! Quit being lazy in your walk with the Lord. What do you think would happen if God decided to go on vacation for a few months? What if he just put his secretary in charge? Come on, people! God wouldn't do that to us, so why are doing it to God?

You think to yourself, *I can sleep with this person; God will forgive me.* Or, *I can curse a few times; it's not like a really bad sin.* We think this even after we know how God feels about these sins. Matthew 5:34–37 says:

> But I tell you, Do not swear at all: either by heaven, for it is God's throne; or by the earth, for it is his footstool; or by Jerusalem, for it is the city of the Great King. And do not swear by your head, for you cannot make even one hair white or black. Simply let your "Yes" be "Yes" and your "No," "No"; anything beyond this comes from the evil one.

Matthew 5:28 addresses the other issue. "But I tell you that anyone who looks at a woman lustfully has already committed adultery with her in his heart." Doing this is taking God's grace for granted. The Lord will judge what you choose to do here on this earth at the appointed time. He knows your heart, and your heart will be judged. Careful! That one time you think you can repent later might not come, for he could demand the life he gave you at anytime.

Let's see what else the Bible has to say about repentance. Luke 3:8–9 says:

> Produce fruit in keeping with repentance. And do not begin to say to yourselves, "We have Abraham as our father." For I tell you that out of these stones God can raise up children for Abraham. The ax is already at the root of the trees, and every tree that does not produce good fruit will be cut down and thrown into the fire.

These words have no flaw. They are straightforward and point blank. If we do not repent from sin and produce good fruit, from my understanding, we will be thrown into the fire. What kind of fire do you think Jesus is talking about? The fire, as I understand it, is hell. Am I wrong? If we as Americans do not repent, God will go to a different nation who will listen and heed his ways. Then he will give his blessings to them, which would otherwise be ours. The previous verse states God can raise children out of stones. Is this what you want? To lose your inheritance? The axe is at your roots; will your tree be chopped down and thrown into the fire?

Luke 5:31–32 says, "It is not the healthy who need a doctor, but the sick. I have not come to call the righteous, but sinners to repentance." There is no hidden agenda in Jesus' words here either. Healthy people do not need a doctor because they are already healthy. Sin is the disease; Jesus is the cure.

God did not send his Son to die on a cross for people who already knew him by his grace. Instead, he sent his son to the ones who did not. I believe God sent Jesus to die on the cross so many would see firsthand with their own eyes the power of God. Then all would have the opportunity to believe through many testimonies about Jesus. Many testimonies confirm truth. We as humans always need to see to believe, so God satisfied our fleshly need with the flesh of his one and only living Son, Jesus Christ!

Looking further at repentance, the Apostle Paul says in Acts 26:20, "First to those in Damascus, then to those in Jerusalem and in all Judea, and to the Gentiles also, I preached that they should repent and turn to God and *prove* their repentance by their deeds." Paul is speaking in his own defense to King Agrippa, the governor, Bernice, and others. At the time Paul was in chains, but the leaders could find no reason to punish him. Expecting to be assassinated anyway, Paul appealed to Caesar and had to be sent to Italy before Caesar. In this passage, Paul is preaching people should repent and turn to God. He does not say you have to, but it says we should. So, here again we see the gift of free will at work, but the ultimate decision is up to you.

You are able to see who has given their lives totally over to Christ by the changes they make in their life. If there is no repentance and change, are we truly saved? Only God knows, but it is a question to you from me, and you can answer that to yourself and to God.

You do not have to repent if you do not want to.

And you might not see any punishment here on earth for your actions. Nevertheless, know that on judgment day, when the book of your life is read and your heart is revealed, you will both see and feel punishment if you're not right with God. Paul said it best in Acts 26:20; prove your repentance by your deeds!

Now, let us head to 2 Corinthians 7:10:

> Godly sorrow brings repentance that leads to salvation and leaves no regret, but worldly sorrow brings death. See what this godly sorrow has produced in you: what earnestness, what eagerness to clear yourselves, what indignation, what alarm, what longing, what concern, what readiness to see justice done.

People, what you read following godly sorrow is *some* fruits of the spirit; there are more.

These fruits of the spirit tend to follow once you ask for your salvation. Godly sorrow, as plainly stated, will lead to salvation, which leaves *no* regret! Regret from what? Your past, present, and future! There is no condemnation from God once you receive your salvation, but you can count on resistance from the evil one. Satan can bring worldly sorrow that can wear you down to the point of death. When you pray for hunger and understanding of God's Word, it amazes me how God answers. After understanding God's principles, how could you live any other way? Repentance leads to life, eternal life!

Next, we will turn to Jeremiah 15:19. "Therefore this is what the Lord says: If you repent, I will restore you that you may serve me; if you utter worthy, not worthless, words, you will be my spokesman." This scripture states that if you repent, the Lord will restore you. He will restore what the devil has stolen from you: emotions, mind, finances, or whatever he has taken. So when you repent from sin, there are rewards. God doesn't ask you to do anything he hasn't already done himself. When you repent, he will use you as a spokesman to glorify his name and his kingdom.

Matthew 4:19 shows how important it is to avoid procrastinating. "Repent, for the kingdom of heaven is near." These words are self-explanatory. How much straighter does God need to get? People, living in sin and thinking that you have time to repent later is a lie from Satan! He tells this lie all the time. What if your life is demanded from you right now? Will there still be *time?* Nope! That would be the end of your book, and you would not know your outcome until the coming and judgment of the Lord.

Luke 13:3 backs this up. "But unless you repent, you too will all perish." Again, Luke 13:5 says the exact same thing. "But unless you repent, you too will all perish." Jesus says this twice within a couple of verses. Do you think he is serious? You bet he is! If the Lord repeats himself, he is trying to get a point across. We need to take the hint and repent. Do these verses need any interpretation? I do not believe so. "But unless you repent, you too will all perish."

Brothers and sisters, we as Christians need to repent, as Hebrews 6:4–6 makes this very clear:

> It is impossible for those who have once been enlightened, who have tasted the heavenly gift, who have shared in the Holy Spirit, who

> have tasted the goodness of the word of God and the powers of the coming age, if they fall away, to be brought back to repentance, because to their loss they are crucifying the son of God all over again and subjecting him to public disgrace.

Did you read that passage carefully? If not, reread it until you understand what it is saying. In short, if you have received salvation and have experienced God's grace and gifts and then you fall away, it will be impossible for you to be brought back to repentance. Because, to your loss, if you have to be brought back to repentance, it would be like you personally nailing Jesus to the cross all over again, making the first time mean nothing. That would be a disgrace to God and the meaning of the cross. Don't you dare put another nail into God's Son! Repent, for the fleshly pleasures will last only a very short period of time. Do not let Satan have control of where you will spend eternity. You have authority over him when Jesus was raised from the dead three days after being placed in the tomb. Use that authority! We only get one sacrifice.

Finally, my last example is from Ezekiel 18:30–32.

> Therefore, O house of Israel, I will judge you, each one according to his ways, declares the Sovereign Lord. Repent! Turn away from all your offences; then sin will not be your downfall. Rid yourselves of all the offences you have committed, and get a new heart and a new spirit. Why will you die, O house of Israel? For I take no pleasure in the death of

anyone, declares the Sovereign Lord. Repent and live!

God pleads through his Son, his Word, and through his prophets. He does not want to send anyone to hell! Nevertheless, many people will give him no choice because they live for what pleased them and not God. I do not know how else to plead with you to repent and make Jesus your Lord and Savior. Everything I have written or tell people is what I have found in God's Word and what the Holy Spirit has revealed to me. Eternity is always right around the corner for us all. Where do you want to spend it? The choice is up to *you!*

Have you ever gone on a trip and needed a road map to get to your destination? Did you ever take a wrong turn, even when you had the map to go by? You see, we have the road map, and that map will lead us to where we need to go, but it is up to us to follow its directions. If you do not follow the directions, you will end up lost and destitute. But if you do follow the directions, that map will lead you to the ultimate destination.

That map is the Holy Bible. To get to a destination, you need to know how to get there! Use the Bible as your map. You will more than likely take some wrong turns, but rest assured, you are not Jesus, and you will never be perfect. That is why the Father sent his only Son to us. We cannot do things in our own strength, but we can in the Father's strength through his only Son!

God's message is simple, so simple that he uses us to preach it. Think about that for a second. His message is *not* complicated, but it does get complicated when the devil comes in to kill, steal, and destroy. That is the only reason why every human will not be saved—because of the selfishness of the devil. You can live two ways: God's way or the devil's way, which is usually your way. There is no in between! Satan's fate is sealed, but if you are reading this book, your fate is yet to be decided, meaning, right now, you are still alive and have time to accept Jesus as your Lord and Savior and to repent from your sins. Repent from what feels good, tastes good, looks good, sounds good, and smells good. Now, don't think I am saying these senses are sin, but these senses could draw you into sin because they are so inviting to our flesh. Sin is foreclosure on your soul. Do not live by your senses, but by the spirit, the Holy Spirit. He dwells in us all who have received Christ. You might need to clean some house to find him, but he *is* there.

What I have written in this book are things you have heard before. I might have a different way of putting words in order, but you have heard them before from other books, people, and your conscience.

Have you ever been doing something you know is wrong and a sense will come over you not to do it? Well, folks, let me introduce you to the whisper of the Holy Spirit. He will leave as quickly as he showed up if you do not want him there. It seems like the only way we learn is when we have to go through tough times and learn the hard way.

Time should be spent in the true Word, God's Word. That is where your knowledge and faith will grow. Learn by surrounding yourself with the Word of God. Repeat as necessary. Repetition should bring the knowledge, and knowledge should lead to repentance!

Remember Luke 13:3: "But unless you repent, you too will all perish."

If you do not know Jesus Christ as your Lord and Savior, but want to know him on a personal basis, say this prayer aloud and from your heart: " Jesus, I come to you as a sinner. I ask you to please forgive my sins and show me where I need to repent. Father God, I believe your Son, Jesus Christ, died on the cross for my sins, and three days later you raised him from the dead. Now he sits at your right hand in the kingdom of heaven. Give me hunger to read your Word and the ability to understand it. I renounce Satan in the name of my Lord and Savior, Jesus Christ, who died for my past and future sins. I repent from known sins, and I ask you to convict me of the unknown ones. Thank you, Father, for your mercy and grace. In Jesus' name, I pray. Amen!"

On judgment day when you stand before the Lord, do not ever say you never had a chance to know about God's mercy, grace, and salvation; you will have no excuses because you have read the words of this book!

Now, may God bless you, and may you bless God and glorify his name!

EPILOGUE: PATIENCE

Well, I am currently thirty-seven years old, and it has been a few years since I wrote this book. I wanted to add this chapter to share some details that has happened over the last few years and why the Lord has had me sit on this book for so long.

A few years ago when I finished this book, I was contacting publishers and had two who were interested. It was a Saturday, and I went and picked up a couple of FedEx envelopes and was putting the addresses of the publishing companies on the front with copies of the book inside, and the Holy Spirit really came upon me. I sensed the Lord wanted me to wait on publishing this book. That really bothered me, and I did not want to accept this. I prayed if it was indeed the Lord speaking to my heart, I really needed him to speak louder and clearer so I would not second-guess him and proceed with my own agenda. Well, he did answer me loud and clear, and I put the book in my safe and have waited the last few years until I heard the Lord give me the okay to proceed.

What the Lord spoke to me was that if I proceeded to pursue a publisher and publish this book that he would indeed bless it, but if I waited on his timing, he would bless it even more. I did not understand then or even now why or even his timing or the extent of the word *blessing;* I just know he spoke, and I no longer questioned him. It was pretty simple. I needed to wait, and I guess I will find out why or not. Either way, I hope and pray for this book to reach many lost souls or even the ones who have currently wandered from their faith during hard times, such as myself.

As I have reread my book, I often thought to myself, *I wish it were as easy as I wrote years ago to get back onto the path of the Lord. What fire I had and will have again, but in time.* When you are on fire for the Lord, things come easy and answers to questions are obvious. But when we are wandering in the desert, it is hard and even more distracting to get back on fire for the Lord. The enemy wants this to happen.

Over the last few years, I found myself cursing a little here and a little there. At first, I thought the words I used were no big deal, but then when I wanted to get my point really across, I used bigger and more demeaning ones. So when you find yourself slipping a little and you think it may be no big deal, it is. The Bible clearly states what the Lord wants from of us. I was also getting very angry at people who wronged me and had hatred toward them as well. First John 2:9 says, "Anyone who claims to be in the light but hates his brother is still in the darkness." So all in all, my light turned into darkness because I got caught up in living in the flesh again. It is hard to volunteer our mistakes, but we are all merely human, and we can receive mercy and grace if we only humble ourselves and ask the Lord to forgive us.

The last couple of years, I met a young lady, and right away, we fell into sin. We were engaged for a while, but the engagement was called off a couple of times for one reason or another, but engagement did not give us the right to do what we did. Marriage is where we have the blessing of the Lord on the subject of sex, not dating or engagement.

I often think, *Why is it so hard? Why do I have to fight so hard for good things? Does God even care about me anymore? Where has he been for all these years? Am I even still saved?* I am sure many Christians have asked questions such as these; I know I am not alone. But the truth of the matter is this: *Why do I make it so hard? Why am I fighting God? Do I even care about God anymore? Where have I been all these years? Am I letting myself be saved?* See, I was projecting all blame and everything I was going through onto God and not myself, where the blame should be in the first place. It's hard to admit, but truth usually is. I think we as Christians think God should answer us in our time and not his. But just maybe there is something to be learned from wandering in the desert. I have not let him work in my heart nor my life, and believe me, he has indeed been trying. I have fought things because I thought I was right for some dumb reason, and that dumb reason is called pride.

The enemy comes in slowly, at a pace that you really don't think at the beginning is a big deal. 1Peter 5:8 says, "Be self-controlled and alert. Your enemy the devil prowls around like a roaring lion looking for someone to devour." '*Prowls*' means sneak; have you ever seen a cat sneak up on its prey? It's very stealthy, just like our enemy. Be careful. He may bring you around people you want a friendship with. Those individuals may curse up a storm, or be sleeping with many partners, or do not believe in God, or who knows what. But I do know that if we choose to hang around people like this, that is indeed whom we will become like. Again, at first you may not even notice a difference, but toward the end or at a crossroad or a rude awakening, you see how a tiny little snowflake has turned into a snowball. Can we blame others for our mistakes? I don't believe we can. More than likely, they did not make you curse or cheat or hate or whatever the sin may be. Yes, we will react to what others do to us, but we do these things all by ourselves. No one else will be sitting with you on judgment day; we need to take responsibilities on what we do, not what others do.

You need to understand, whoever we invite into our lives or homes, we invite their spiritual warfare as well into our lives. Have you ever had overwhelming feelings or thoughts such as, suicide, lust, hate, anger, depression, or fear, to name a few? Yup, if you normally do not have these kinds of feelings, you may have been around someone who does, and your spirit picked up on those things and made you feel the same as them. Or you could be the one carrying these feelings due to something that has caused you much pain. But if you are in tune to the Holy Spirit and have an understanding of the authority Jesus has given us all, you can rebuke it and pray for those people. It also depends on the kind of TV or movies you watch as well. We invite things into our homes and lives all the time through the people we hang around and the entertainment we let into our minds and homes. It is real.

I may want to have had this book published years

ago, and yes, I may have wanted to have a wife and family by now, but what good does it do to wish on things you do not have? It actually is called coveting, and yes, that is a sin. So as I write these last few words of this book and before I ship it off to the publisher's, I am reminded God does still love me, and he has not forgotten his promises to me. For example, it is very hard for a new author to get published. I sent this book in one time and it was accepted. Praise Jesus! Not because of me, but because when God answers prayers, no matter how impossible they seem to you or others, he answers in a way you know it is him working in your life. That is exciting! These days, I am really starting to understand God's mercy and grace on a whole new level, and it is very humbling.

When I wrote this book a few years ago, I really prided myself that I was doing a great job for the Lord and I was really on track with my life, and I wondered at that time, *Why is it so hard for others to do the same?* I set myself up for my fall and a wandering in the desert, looking back in hindsight. Romans 3:22–24 says: "This righteousness from God comes through faith in Jesus Christ to all who believe. There is no difference, for all have sinned and fall short of the glory of God, and are justified freely by his grace through the redemption that came by Christ Jesus." So wondering what I wondered, I was wrong and being judgmental. The key words in this scripture, I believe, are *all, justified,* and *freely.* We need to be careful about judging others, but pay more attention to judging ourselves and praying to the Lord on how we can make ourselves better.

So, back to patience. This term is so hard for me, as well as many others, to put into action. You see, we all want to put action into this term, but the only kind of actions needing to be put into this term is waiting, faith, and being still. Yup, those sorts of actions are tough, aren't they? We want the kind of action that sees results in seconds and minutes, not months and years. Am I alone? More than likely not. So during my time out in the desert, I have been tested, tempted, and discouraged. Those are the enemy's tactics, not God's. But God does watch how we react during our time of trials. So what you may be praying for, maybe you are not ready yet, but you need to be refined, like gold. God needs us to be pure, in a way of speaking, in a way that we will be ready for those blessings we are praying for. Answered prayers generally will bring a responsibility we may not be ready for. For me, that's why I believe I have not received what I have prayed for. Maybe I was not ready to be an author or have a family or be married yet. I don't know, but I do believe things happen for a reason, and during the process, I have to stay focused on being patient and wait on his timing and not expect things to be done on my timing. Having patience and seeking the Lord's guidance will get us ready for the responsibility to follow at a fast pace. Therefore, try to be patient and do not just rely on yourself. Pray and ask for direction. In time, you will get the direction you need to go in, but most often it is never our time or direction, but his time and his direction, and I wouldn't want it any other way.

> Lord, I humbly come before you and ask for the ones who read this book to be blessed in the way that you need them to be blessed. I ask you to encourage people who may have

fallen short because the enemy has beat them up with lies, like he did me. I bind and rebuke those lies in Jesus' name and take full authority you have given us, and cast them back to the pits of hell. Keep your children safe in these end days, Lord. Give us revelations of your will for each and every one of our lives. Speak to the ones who have doubt about you, oh Lord, and encourage them in some way so they may really know you are alive and well today and now. Bless your children! Bless us so we may bless others! Prepare us for what you have already prepared for us! In Jesus' name, I pray. Amen!

e|LIVE

---

listen|imagine|view|experience

AUDIO BOOK DOWNLOAD INCLUDED WITH THIS BOOK!

In your hands you hold a complete digital entertainment package. In addition to the paper version, you receive a free download of the audio version of this book. Simply use the code listed below when visiting our website. Once downloaded to your computer, you can listen to the book through your computer's speakers, burn it to an audio CD or save the file to your portable music device (such as Apple's popular iPod) and listen on the go!

How to get your free audio book digital download:

1. Visit www.tatepublishing.com and click on the e|LIVE logo on the home page.
2. Enter the following coupon code: 8b04-ae50-bd09-9f77-9f81-7db4-08d9-2d53
3. Download the audio book from your e|LIVE digital locker and begin enjoying your new digital entertainment package today!